LOVE AFFAIR

LOVE AFFAIR

by Alfred Shaughnessy
adapted from *Coup de Soleil* by Marcel Mithois

LONDON

A member of the Chappell and Intersong Music Group

First published 1985 by
ETG, English Theatre Guild Ltd,
129 Park Street, London W1Y 3FA.

© Copyright Alfred Shaughnessy 1985

ISBN 0 85676 016 1

Typeset and printed by Commercial Colour Press, London E7.
Cover design by Robin Lowry.

LOVE AFFAIR was first presented at the Theatre Royal, Brighton, on 1 October 1984, with the following cast.

VALENTINE MATIGNON	Sian Phillips
PATRICK CROISSET	Robin Sachs
GHISLAINE	Pauline Bennion
JEAN CARMEREC	Anthony Higginson
GERARD LENOTRE	Moray Watson
JEROME	Alan Colhoun
BRIGITTE MONTILLIER	Anne Lawson

Directed by Charles Savage
Designed by Stuart Stanley

The Play is set in Paris in the Spring of 1925.

The action takes place in Valentine Matignon's top floor apartment in an elegant house in the fashionable Rue de Varenne.

ACT I

Scene 1	Early evening, Tuesday.
Scene 2	The next morning, and later that day.

ACT II

Scene 1	The next morning, Thursday.
Scene 2	A few days later, 8 pm.

photo by Richard Wintle, from the original production of Love Affair.

ACT ONE

Scene One

The scene throughout is the lower half of VALENTINE MATIGNON'S *maisonette, occupying the top two floors of an elegant eighteenth century house in the Rue de Varenne, Paris. It is early spring, 1925.*

Upstairs left is the kitchen with a serving hatch, and left are some stairs up to the bedrooms. Upstage right is the entrance door. On shelves around the apartment are a collection of ornate bottles, old and new, containing perfume, eau de cologne and toilet water. The furniture is a tasteful mixture of Edwardian and Art Deco. The colour scheme is salmon pink and white. There is a small writing desk with a telephone on it and a swivel chair to the side.

On the top level of the apartment, a landing connects the bedroom with the bathroom, where anyone passing across will be in full view of the living room and audience. The use of an upper level is however optional. The play can be performed on one level, with the bedroom and bathroom exits upstage left as indicated on the set plan (see back of playscript).

As the curtain rises, GHISLAINE, VALENTINE'S *young maid is laying dinner for two on a small table, downstage right.*

GHISLAINE   (*Laying table*) Wine glass for Monsieur Gérard, wine glass for Madame. Knife for Monsieur Gérard, knife for Madame. Fork for Monsieur Gérard, fork for Madame. There, (*calling off*). The table's ready.

           VALENTINE *enters from the kitchen. She is an attractive, smart Parisienne in her fifties.*

VALENTINE   (*Entering from kitchen*) Thank you Ghislaine. (*She sees two spoons not laid out and lays them on the table*) And it's a spoon for Monsieur Gérard and a spoon for Madame. Not just 'spoons' for anybody in particular. (VALENTINE *sighs*).

GHISLAINE   Oh dear, silly me! What's the matter Madame? Aren't you looking forward to your evening?

           GHISLAINE *puts on her coat to go*

VALENTINE   (*With a shrug*) I don't know. I suppose I am.

GHISLAINE   Have you gone off him?

VALENTINE   You don't just go off someone after fifteen
             years. Do you know Ghislaine, I was working it
             out in my bath, tonight will be my 795th
             candle-lit dinner in this apartment with
             Monsieur Gérard. And frankly, I don't think I
             can face another.

GHISLAINE   But Madame, you're all made-up and dressed
             and you look so elegant. Here let me light the
             candle before you change your mind. You'll
             soon get in the mood. You know, warm up after
             a few glasses of wine and everything (GHISLAINE
             lights three candles). There! I'll see you on
             Thursday.

             GHISLAINE *goes out.* VALENTINE *ponders. Then.*

VALENTINE   (*Puffing out the candles*) No, no, no, not tonight or
             ever again. This has got to stop. Now. (*She
             removes the other mat and glass from the table. Then
             she goes to fetch a writing pad and pen from the desk.
             Sits to write. Writing*) Dear Gérard, I am writing
             to tell you that I'm sick to death of our endless
             and quite futile affair ... Gérard darling, I feel
             that I need a change of climate. That's more
             like a weather forecast. Dearest Gérard, you
             know that ... Oh God. (*To audience*) The
             trouble with me is that I'm much too much of a
             coward to break it to his face. You see my old
             and faithful lover is on his way back from
             Geneva, and I don't know how to tell him it's
             all over. Its not only him I'm tired of, I'm tired
             of us. The dreary couple we've become, when
             he visits me three nights a week. I don't want
             him to change, he's a dear, and marvellous
             company, intelligent, thoughtful, always the
             same. He's been 'always the same' for fifteen
             years, but at our age ... what does it all add up
             to? Love? We shall end up like a dreary old
             married couple, flipping through a faded
             photograph album. That's what he does, every
             time he comes here, flips through my
             photograph album. God how I hate photograph
             albums! It's living in the past. The horror of

seeing yourself looking divinely young in clothes that are by now hideously dated. Then you shut the wretched album, glance at yourself in the mirror and there you are back in the present looking every bit your age. No, no, give me the future every time. 'Is that all she's got against him' I can hear you say. The fact that he likes looking at old photographs? Yes, you're quite right, its all my fault. (*Resumes writing*) What's happened to us, Gérard darling, is that cosiness and habit have crept up on our passion, every Tuesday, Thursday and Saturday. (*To audience*) It's Tuesday today, maybe I'll stick it out 'til Thursday. No, not even until Thursday. Oh I don't know, I need time to think. (*Writing*) I have made up mind to end it now. Love and kisses dearest, I do mean that. Your Valentine. P.S. I am not leaving you for another man, because there is no other man. P.P.S. Cold beef and Aspic in the refrigerator. (*The bell rings*). There! Its too late. Oh God! Ah well, I'll just have to postpone my escape until Thursday. (*Another ring at the door*) All right, all right, I've been waiting for you for three weeks, can't you wait one second for me?

She goes to open the door. To her surprise there stands a young man, PATRICK CROISSET, *in an overcoat and beret. He is very puffed and clutches a bouquet of flowers which is unwrapped. Unable to speak, he makes for a chair and flops down in it, gasping for breath.*

PATRICK   (*Breathless*) So sorry, just let me ... get my breath back ... oh dear ... your lift was at the top floor and ... someone ... left the gate open. Had to ... walk all the way up ...

VALENTINE   What do you want?

PATRICK   (*Handing her the bouquet*) Give you ... this.

            VALENTINE, *suspicious, does not take it, but backs away from him.*

VALENTINE   Who are you?

PATRICK   Rose Petal.

VALENTINE	I beg your pardon?
PATRICK	Rose . . . Petal.
VALENTINE	(*Baffled*) Oh.
PATRICK	Rose Petal is a shop. A florist.
VALENTINE	Ah! I say, those narcissi smell quite divine. Such fragrance.
PATRICK	Don't tell me you can smell them from over there.
VALENTINE	Of course I can. I'm a 'nose'.
PATRICK	A what?
VALENTINE	A 'nose'. I'm one of those people with a highly developed sense of smell, so I work for a perfume manufacturer, sampling and balancing ingredients, mixing together different flavours and creating scent. That's my profession.
PATRICK	Interesting kind of nose to have.
VALENTINE	My nose is more than just interesting, young man. Every sniff it takes is worth a great deal of money. Chanel would give her eyeteeth for the use of my nose and so would Worth.

She takes the bouquet from PATRICK *and is about to put it in a vase.*

PATRICK	(*Quickly*) Oh my God no, not in that vase. (VALENTINE *stops*) It's hideous and much too small. They'll suffocate in that monstrosity. (*He points to a larger vase*) Put 'em in that one.
VALENTINE	(*Doing so*) You prefer this one, do you? Good, it happens to be my trophy from the perfume industry as the best 'nose' in Paris 1924. Do you normally deliver flowers unwrapped?
PATRICK	I can't bear suffocating them in cellophane. Flowers like to inhale you know, and to be inhaled. I enjoyed their scent all the way here.
VALENTINE	Who sent them? I can't see a card.
PATRICK	There isn't one. We got an Interflora message with the order from Geneva. I jotted it down.

(*He consults a piece of paper in his pocket and reads*)
'Missed connection at Vallorbe. No train until
tommorow. Love and kisses (in the plural).
Gérard.'

VALENTINE   (*With a smile*) Oh, I see, well . . . .

She finds a banknote in her bag and offers it to
PATRICK, *moving towards the still open front door.*

PATRICK   (*Seeing the tip*) Look, if that is a tip you're
offering me, please don't. *I'm* the florist, and it's
my shop. I just thought it might be fun to make
up the bouquet myself since the shop was closed,
both the girls gone, all nice and quiet. I was
totting up the cash register when the order came
through from Geneva. So I made up the
bouquet myself for love of the gentle art of
flower arrangement, and brought it round here
myself for the love of fresh air and exercise, and
now I deliver it to you for the love of giving
pleasure.

VALENTINE   How charming. Your bouquet is exquisite.
Beautifully blended. Lovely pastel shades. (*She
places a petal on the back of her hand and sniffs it*)
Curious, isn't it, how the little tea rose actually
smells of tea? (*She looks at him*) Well, Thank you
for my flowers, I'm really very touched. I mean,
why should you work so hard and so late for
me? I'd offer you some refreshment if only I . . .

PATRICK   (*Coming quickly into the flat*) Thank you very
much.

VALENTINE *shrugs and goes to close the front door.*
Patrick edges his way futher into the apartment.

PATRICK   I'd love a drink, if you have time. I thought I
sensed you were about to go out when I . . .

VALENTINE   Oh, yes, well, I . . . not really, no. Whisky?

PATRICK   (*shuddering*) oh God no.

VALENTINE   Sorry. Wine . . . Muscadet? There's a new
bottle in the fridge ready for . . . (*She stops herself
and disappears into the kitchen from where she continues*

speaking) Are you good at opening bottles? I usually finish up drenched from head to foot in Claret, with half the cork still firmly in the bottle. A corkscrew is not enough for me (*We hear a pop*) I need an umbrella and a pair of eyebrow tweezers.

VALENTINE *comes out with a bottle of wine and two glasses. She pours the wine, and mutters to herself.*

VALENTINE   Do you know, I think I might stay in this evening, after all, and enjoy these lovely flowers, your lovely flowers, his lovely flowers.

PATRICK *glances at the table.*

PATRICK   I take it the other place at your table is for Gérard?

VALENTINE   (*Embarrassed*) Well, yes, as a matter of fact ...

PATRICK   (*Making to clink glasses*) Santé Madame.

VALENTINE   (*Clinking her glass*) Santé, Monsieur.

A silence. They sip their wine.

PATRICK   Might I sit down?

VALENTINE   Please do.

PATRICK   (*sitting*) And what about the other one?

VALENTINE   What other what?

PATRICK   The other place at the table. For you?

VALENTINE   Yes, but ... well, to be honest I'd just decided not to dine in this evening. It's rather a long story, of no possible interest to you. (PATRICK *laughs heartily*) Why are you laughing?

PATRICK   I think it's highly comical.

VALENTINE   What is?

PATRICK   I arrive here with flowers from your Gérard, at the precise moment that you decide to walk out on him. I think that's a scream.

VALENTINE *looks at him horrified.*

VALENTINE   Is it your habit to indulge in impudent conversation like this?

PATRICK	Yes, and to prove it I'm going to put an impudent proposition to you.
VALENTINE	(*Guarded*) What?
PATRICK	(*Nodding to the table*) That Patrick, that's me by the way, Patrick takes the place of your Gérard at your dinner table this evening and, later on, in your bed.

PATRICK *now relaxes on the sofa.*

VALENTINE	Do you mind saying that again?
PATRICK	Not in the least. Patrick takes the place of Gérard at the table and in the bed, for tonight, and, who knows, for how many more nights. Yes?

VALENTINE *strides over to* PATRICK, *snatches his glass from his hand and shows him the door.*

VALENTINE	Clear out!
PATRICK	(*Smiling*) Oh dear. You're not half as outraged as I hoped you'd be. I wanted you to say 'Sir, I am not that kind of woman'. What a shame. Never mind.
VALENTINE	Please go!
PATRICK	Why? Is there something off-putting about me?
VALENTINE	Yes there is. Your boorish behaviour, for one thing.
PATRICK	What else?
VALENTINE	I happen to dislike being made a fool of.
PATRICK	Oh, come on, I wasn't trying to make a fool of you. What makes you think that? Is it because I'm thirty and you're 50ish? Are you 50ish?
VALENTINE	Let us just say that every day I find myself slipping further away from 40ish. Now, would you mind leaving.
PATRICK	Oh please let me stay a minute longer.
VALENTINE	Get out, or I'll call the police.
PATRICK	You may be sure, Madame, and possibly a little disappointed, that I do not intend to ravish you.

VALENTINE	I should think not indeed. From the look of you, I doubt if you've got the strength. You *could* be planning to rob me, of course, it has been known, people ringing bells and pretending to deliver flowers.
PATRICK	Come on, do I look like a burglar? All right, I admit I behaved like a cad. I just thought you seemed a bit down in the mouth. Rather depressed. So I said to myself, let's go for broke. She'll either throw me out on my ear, or she'll say 'please stay and dine with me'. Alas, in my excitement, I added the bed to the place at the table, and that was a grave mistake, for which I apologise. Now, if I'd invited you to dine with me this evening, tête à tête, at a restaurant, what would you've said, be honest?
VALENTINE	I'd have said 'I'm sorry, but I can think of a number of friends I can dine with tonight, if I wished to go out'. I don't happen to know you, nor do I have the remotest desire to extend our acquaintance. Does that answer your question?
PATRICK	Come on, don't tell me you're that conventional.
VALENTINE	Now, look here, young man ...
PATRICK	My name is Patrick, I thought I'd told you. Certain people I know who love me, call me Patonnet.
VALENTINE	(*Pointing to the door*) Oh for God's sake go!
PATRICK	Tell me what poor Gérard was getting for his dinner tonight, if he'd arrived? Go on, what's on the menu?
VALENTINE	That's none of your business. Now, out you go.
PATRICK	My God, my flowers! Must put them in water.
	PATRICK *picks up the flowers and rushes into the kitchen.*
VALENTINE	(*To herself, sniffing the air*) I was wrong, its not Tea Rose, its rotting leaf mould.

PATRICK   (*Coming in again*) Oh Madame, Cold Beef in Aspic. Whoever told you it's my favourite dish?

VALENTINE   Goodbye.

               PATRICK *falls to his kness, hands together in mock supplication.*

PATRICK   Dear, kind lady. Plese don't send me away. Be generous, be compassionate, be of a noble spirit and share your Cold Beef in Aspic with a hungry young man, who's just walked all the way along the Boulevard Raspail to bring you a bouquet of flowers. Be my Valentine!

VALENTINE   How did you know I was called Valentine?

PATRICK   The message from Interflora was for a Madame Valentine Matignon of 30 rue de Varenne. Oh, but Cold Beef in Aspic, God, how I love it, more than anything else in the world.

VALENTINE   So does Gérard. Now stop making an idiot of yourself, get up off your knees, and depart.

PATRICK   (*Getting up again*) Alright, I will, but you'll regret it one of these days. You'll kick yourself for abandoning what might have been a very pleasant little interlude in our lives. Pity. Ah, well, when you next require flowers, remember the most beautiful rare blooms from the whole of Europe are to be found at the Rose Petal flower shop in the rue Miguel.

               PATRICK *opens the door to go.*

VALENTINE   Just a minute . . .

               PATRICK *closes the door and is quickly back in the room again.*

PATRICK   I've won, haven't I? Do you know, I had a bet with myself you wouldn't chuck me out.

VALENTINE   You may give me the address of your flower shop.

PATRICK   No need. The Rose Petal is listed in every shopping guide and directory in Paris, so please think of a better reason for asking me to stay.

VALENTINE	(*Resigned*) Alright, you may stay and help me dispose of the Cold Beef in Aspic, on one condition.
PATRICK	I can't promise to treat you with the reverence and respect due to your age. Nor can I undertake not to talk nonsense. You must expect me to be outrageous because I am notoriously outrageous.

PATRICK *crashes to the floor and lies on his back.* VALENTINE *laughs.*

VALENTINE	Do you wish your Beef in Aspic served to you down there?
PATRICK	(*Getting up again*) I shall outrage you Valentine, I warn you.
VALENTINE	Don't worry, I have a reputation for taming wild men. You should see me at the perfume laboratory.
PATRICK	Oh, I can. Sniffing about with that famous 'nose' of yours.

VALENTINE *shrugs her shoulders and goes off to the kitchen.*

VALENTINE	(*As she goes*) Now you can stop the chatter, put that mat and wine glass back on the table, while I get some bread and a few gherkins.

VALENTINE *goes off to the kitchen.*

PATRICK	Tell me, is your Gérard amusing?
VALENTINE	(*From the kitchen*) Amusing hardly describes my Gérard.

VALENTINE *now comes in again, with a tray. He helps her with it.*

PATRICK	It describes you all right.
VALENTINE	You think so? Why?
PATRICK	It's something I read in your eyes. A kind of smouldering mischief that only needs the slightest puff to kindle the flame, and it's not only in your eyes. If you weren't an amusing

person, you'd never have asked me to stay. What's more, if I hadn't suspected you had a sense of fun, I'd never have dared to say what I did, or to have played this particular card.

VALENTINE   Well, you can stop dealing the cards, sit down and eat your dinner like a properly brought up young man.

She sits down at the table. PATRICK *bows and scrapes and holds her chair for her.*

PATRICK   (*Fooling*) Very good Madame. Thank you Madame. After you Madame. A little wine Madame? My pleasure Madame.

VALENTINE *jerks her head, irritated by this childish performance. As she drinks her wine, she stares at* PATRICK, *who now sits down beside her.*

PATRICK   I say, must you look at me like that? Its rather intimidating.

VALENTINE   Me, intimidate you? Impossible. If I don't look just a little formidable, who knows what further demands you might make of me, apart from dinner and bed.

PATRICK   I'll tell you.

VALENTINE   What?

PATRICK   A kiss.

VALENTINE   Look, I'm well aware of my limitations as a woman, and its really not very kind of you to make fun of me, when I'm old enough to be your mother.

PATRICK   But ...

VALENTINE   Don't 'but' me. I could be your mother ... well, almost.

PATRICK   Age means nothing to me, I promise you.

VALENTINE   Well, it does to me. Whenever I peer at myself in the mirror, that cruel, distorting, enlarging mirror, I can see a thousand little wrinkles all around my eyes.

PATRICK   Shut up! Don't talk like that!

VALENTINE	And you shut up! I know what I am and what I look like.
PATRICK	So do I. Shall I tell you? You look appetizing and tempting, like a delicious brioche, oven-warm and spread with honey; to be enjoyed in bed for breakfast.
VALENTINE	Patrick, dear, let us get one thing quite straight. If the day every comes when I decide to take on a gigolo, it certainly won't be you.
PATRICK	(*Laughing*) A gigolo? Me? A kept boy? With a rich mistress. My dear woman, do you imagine I'm impressed by this very ordinary little apartment of yours? I'll bet I'm a damn sight richer than you are.
VALENTINE	Oh, you think so, do you?
PATRICK	I know I am. Just because your sixty . . .
VALENTINE	(*Quickly*) Who said I was?
PATRICK	(*Calmly*) . . . just because your sixty square foot living room may be nicely furnished, it's nothing compared with the rather grand six-bedroomed house with a large garden that I inherited from my mother.
VALENTINE	Six bedrooms? Really? (*Pause*) I don't wish to be inquisitive, but do you live in a house of that size . . . all on your own?
PATRICK	Not all the time.
VALENTINE	Oh.
PATRICK	(*Laughing*) There, I knew it. You're dying of curiosity, aren't you? I can see it in your eyes: 'Is he married? Divorced? A transvestite? A bigamist? Impotent? A sadist, perhaps? Or simply a chaser after anything in skirts'. Can you guess? Well, I won't keep you in suspense any longer. The truth is that I'm . . .
VALENTINE	(*Interrupting*) No, don't bother. I'm not remotely interested in your secret vices.

A silence. PATRICK *smiles.*

VALENTINE	Yes, I am. What are they?
PATRICK	(*Taking her hand*) My life, Chapter 1 . . .
VALENTINE	(*Letting go of his hand, rising and going out to the kitchen*) I don't think I can sit through your life story without more to eat, so I'll fetch the chocolate mousse. It's the only thing Ghislaine doesn't make a total hash of. Meanwhile, you can fill up my glass.

PATRICK *does so, then he quickly places the two chairs closer together at the table.* VALENTINE *returns with the chocolate mousse and some biscuits and sits down again.* PATRICK *sticks his finger in the mousse to sample it.*

PATRICK	Mmm! 'Bueno, bueno'. Who's Ghislaine?
VALENTINE	Oh, come on, that's disgusting.
PATRICK	(*Licking his finger*) Who is Ghislaine?
VALENTINE	My maid.
PATRICK	That's a pretty grand name for a maid.

VALENTINE, *who has noticed the new position of the chairs, does not sit down.*

VALENTINE	It is rather. Her mother was my dressmaker and the child desparately needs money. She goes to an art school. In her time off between the drawing lessons which she gets free in exchange for a little modelling, she comes here to me, where she is quite, quite useless. Unfortunately, her mother died and her lover deserted her with a four month old baby.
PATRICK	Poor girl. Like my mama. Well, she was married, but Papa left her a few days after I was born and pushed off to South America. My poor mother had to go out to work to feed and educate me.
VALENTINE	As a domestic servant?
PATRICK	As a whore. She was on the game all her life. She was a great beauty, my mama.
VALENTINE	I'm sure she was.

PATRICK *has come back to* VALENTINE.

PATRICK	I meant everything to her, you know. She adored me, spoilt me, cosseted me and, frankly, corrupted me. I was always locked in her arms. Do you know, from the day papa left us I always slept in her bed. She used to stroke me and call me her little chick and her baby doll.
VALENTINE	I'm amazed you aren't as queer as a coot.
PATRICK	(*Quite naturally*) Oh I was, until a woman friend of my mother's straightened me out, if you know what I mean.
VALENTINE	Ah, that explains everything.
PATRICK	What does it explain?
VALENTINE	I remind you of your mother's woman friend, who straightened you out.
PATRICK	Oh no, you remind me of my mother's woman friend's daughter.

VALENTINE *looks flattered.*

VALENTINE	Do I?

(*A pause*)

PATRICK	Now what about your life story, come on, it's your turn.
VALENTINE	My life? Very simple. I've never 'changed course' like you. I simply marrried young to escape from a dull bourgeios family. At 23, I was widowed by a motor accident. After that I had various affairs, mostly trivial. Then one night, at a boring dinner party, I found myself sitting next to Gérard Lenotre. When it was time to go home, I said I'd like a taxi and he offered to get one and share it with me. It was the old, old story. When we got to my place here, it was pouring with rain. I rather liked him, so I invited him up for nightcap and to borrow an umbrella, as he was going to walk home from here . . . his apartment is just round the corner. The following evening, he brought the umbrella back and stayed for another drink. I found him distinctly attractive and, that was it.

Now, today, after fifteen years, it's different.
We understand each other, rather too well.
We've plenty in common, same taste in most
things, same opinions. We never discuss
anything very profound. It's the same with most
couples really ... too much agreement and
harmony leading to monotony and boredom. Do
you know there are times when I long for a
damn good row.

PATRICK   (*Suddenly flaring up*) Oh, God! How can you be
so naive, really, to stand there and tell me that
harmony breeds monotony. Rot and rubbish. It
just isn't true. I don't think I can listen to any
more of this. I'm going home.

VALENTINE *stands there stultified by this outburst.*

PATRICK   (*Like an advert*) That one-and-a-half seconds of
'damn good row' came to you by the courtesy of
Rose Petal, the only florist in Paris, who can
provide an extra service with the flowers. Rows
and Roses for you from Rose Petal. (PATRICK
sits down, smiling) This mousse is delicious. Tell
me, what does Gérard do for a living?

VALENTINE   He's an architect; designing and building chalets
for holiday-makers in the Swiss Alps.

PATRICK   Fifteen years, eh? That's a long time to be 'en
menage' with someone.

VALENTINE   Thank you.

PATRICK   Come on, Valentine, let's see you smile (*she
smiles*). Now that we know everything about each
other ...

PATRICK *puts a hand out to take her by the arm.*

VALENTINE   (*Backing away*) No, no. I haven't told you how
they discovered my 'nose' (VALENTINE *gets up and
paces about the apartment trying to regain her poise*)
Would it not interest you to know how they
discovered my nose for perfume?

PATRICK   No.

VALENTINE   No?

PATRICK   No.

VALENTINE   That's a shame because I'm dying to know what
            made you take up floristry.

            PATRICK *takes a swallow of wine, gets up and moves
            towards her, she steps back.*

PATRICK   You don't really want to know but I'm going to
            tell you all the same. I've never passed a single
            exam in my life. The only thing I ever knew was
            how to grow and arrange flowers. Avoiding all
            forms of tedious study, I lived for many years in
            comfort and luxury off the immoral earnings of
            my mother. When she died, ten years ago, she
            left me all her money and jewellery, with the
            proceeds of which I bought my flower shop. It
            had been a delicatessen store, specialising in
            particularly strong cheeses. It took me three
            months to get rid of the stink and do the place
            up; then I opened to an astonished and
            enthusiastic public, as the Rose Petal. (PATRICK
            looks at her defiantly) There, now you know.

VALENTINE   (*Anxiously trying to avoid him*) And your flowers
            ... do you ... buy in every day from the
            market or? ...

PATRICK   Not very often. I get most of my supplies direct
            from nurseries in France, Germany, Holland,
            Asia, Puerto Rico, the Canaries, Burma,
            Manchester, Oldham ...

            PATRICK *comes nearer and nearer to her.* VALENTINE
            is becoming tempted. She looks at PATRICK, *he looks
            hard at her. A pause.*

VALENTINE   (*Of the table*) I'll have to clear away. Ghislaine
            isn't coming tommorow

            VALENTINE *moves to the table. In a flash,* PATRICK
            has her round the waist.

PATRICK   No, don't.

VALENTINE   Let go of me.

PATRICK   No.

            VALENTINE *disengages a hand and manages to slap his
            face hard.* PATRICK *remains, for a second, stunned.*

VALENTINE   Oh, dear, I'm sorry.

PATRICK, furious, is about to pick up the large vase with his flowers in it and smash it down on her head, but he hesitates, puts it down and takes a rose from the vase, puts it in the buttonhole of his jacket on a chair, which he now puts on again, moving towards the door.

PATRICK   Thank you for my tip, Madame ... I refer, of course, to the Cold Beef in Aspic, the chocolate mousse and the Muscadet. All quite delicious. Good night, Madame. It's been a pleasure.

PATRICK puts his hand on the door handle. It stays there. The lights fade.

Scene Two

The same, next morning. On the table are remnants of breakfast for two; coffee pot, cups, marmalade, etc. VALENTINE, in her pyjamas, is doing exercises to keep herself in trim. She has a curious smile on her face as she moves to address the audience, while PATRICK walks by, from the bedroom, almost naked, on his way to the bathroom.

VALENTINE   I'm a sick woman, that's what I am, but, mind you, there are plenty of other women with my particular sickness. Oh, yes. What about all those women in novels and plays and films with lovers younger than themselves, but fancy me, of all people. I know what you're going to say, when it all comes to an end that poor woman's in for a dreadful let-down. She'll come tumbling down from a great height. Too bad. So I'll tumble. But at least I'll have been up there, floating on air for a while and it's going to be marvellous, while it lasts. You see, the trouble is, I'd quite forgotten what it was like to be in love. I remember now, alright. It's rather like ballooning, soaring free over the mountains and villages and across the valleys, everything down below looking so small and insiginficant. I don't mind telling you, I really am rather surprised at myself ... Oh, yes, I am. And ... yes I can

hear you whispering to each other out there:
you're saying: 'That woman is quite without
shame'. Of course I'm ashamed of myself.
There I am one evening, with no appetite,
facing a stale old piece of Cold Beef in Aspic,
and what happens? An angel passes by and, ooh
lala, my appetite is miraculously appeased. In a
flash, I've snatched that little passing angel out
of the air and devoured him raw, wings, feathers
and all. Oh, yes, I'm ashamed of myself alright;
but it is rather fun.

We hear a key turn in the lock. GHISLAINE, *the maid
comes in.*

VALENTINE   Ghislaine? What are you doing here today, it's
not Thursday. You came yesterday.

As she speaks, GHISLAINE *puts down her shoulder bag
and takes out a decorative little housecoat which she puts
on over her dress. Then she swaps her high-heeled shoes
for slippers and ties a scarf on her head.*

GHISLAINE   I know, Madame. I hope you don't mind, but
you see a photographer friend's going to take
some photos of my baby tomorrow. It's for a
competition in the newspapers, for bonny
babies. Well, I know little Alphonse has got a
squint but I thought he just might win it. Isn't it
suitable if I come today?

At this moment, PATRICK *appears, more or less naked,
on his way from the bedroom to the bathroom. Only*
GHISLAINE *sees him. She stares at him, transfixed.*

VALENTINE   No, it's just that I'd planned to stay home today
and work at my desk. It doesn't matter.

A pause. GHISLAINE *is still looking at him, her mouth
wide open.*

GHISLAINE   Warm for the time of year, isn't it?

GHISLAINE *giggles, but not* VALENTINE, *who is 'far
away'.*

GHISLAINE   What's the matter, Madame? Aren't you feeling
well this morning?

VALENTINE	Not very. I lied to you just now, Ghislaine. I'm going to take the day off. I phoned the laboratory just now to say I wouldn't be going in.
GHISLAINE	Oh. So you are ill?
VALENTINE	Not exactly ill. I just feel as though I was being gripped round my ankles and wrists and my neck by an iron fist. I feel sort of paralysed. Quite numb. But not ill.

VALENTINE *picks up a sort of mixing bowl and wooden spoon and starts to stir mechanically.*

GHISLAINE	(*Sniffing*) What are you mixing Madame? Is it a souffle? I can smell eggs.
VALENTINE	That's right. Egg, cucumber and soda water. (*she points to her face*) Something to stimulate the skin a little ... Well, all right, get the creases out.
GHISLAINE	I see (*She is by the table*). Just what *is* going on here Madame? Coffee for two? Don't tell me Monsieur Gérard's given up his China tea and milk for black coffee; or has M. Gérard turned into ... someone else? (*She glances towards the bedroom*).

PATRICK *now leaves the bathroom with a towel round his middle.* VALENTINE *still hasn't seen him, but* GHISLAINE *has.*

VALENTINE	That's right, Ghislaine, someone else; someone quite ... else. You've no idea how else. All right, I'll come clean and tell you. You see, last night ... (*The bell rings and interrupts her*).
GHISLAINE	(*Annoyed*) There now.
VALENTINE	Be an angel and see who that is. If it's for me, I'm out. If it's more flowers, tell them I've run out of vases. (VALENTINE *goes into her bedroom*).
GHISLAINE	(*Still reeling from her glimpse of* PATRICK) Ooh, Madame. Quelle surprise!

GHISLAINE *goes over to open the door. A man with a suitcase hurries in muttering to himself. It is* MONSIEUR CARMAREC.

CARMAREC	(*Assuming it is* VALENTINE *who has opened the door*) There are some things no human being worthy of the name should be allowed to ... (*He stops, seeing* GHISLAINE) ... Who the devil are you?
GHISLAINE	I'm the maid. And who the devil are you?
CARMAREC	My name is Jean Carmarec, and I'm your employer's employer. I don't believe for one moment you *are* the maid here; you don't sound like a maid; but I've neither the time nor the inclination to find out who you are, so run along and fetch your mistress, if you please.
GHISLAINE	She's not in.
CARMAREC	Very well, I'll wait.
GHISLAINE	She may not be coming back.
CARMAREC	(*Sitting down*) We'll see.

VALENTINE *now comes out of her bedroom, making a sign of irritation with her head to* GHISLAINE. GHISLAINE *shrugs, indicating 'I did my best', then she goes into the kitchen with another shrug as if to say 'what else could I do?'*

VALENTINE	Alright, Ghislaine, thank you.
CARMAREC	As I was about to say, my dear Valentine, there are some things no human being worthy of the name should be allowed to do to another human being.
VALENTINE	I was about to say the same thing to you. You have absolutely no right to come barging in ...
CARMAREC	(*Interrupting her*) Valentine, my precious Valentine, are you trying to ruin me ... to ruin us? We're miles behind schedule with the perfume project; our chief competitors have already presented their formula to Riccis and I hear it is quite excellent. Now what about us? You haven't been near the laboratory for weeks. You know it's crucial for us to get our formula in tomorrow. The other manufacturers will beat us to it, and none of them has a quarter of your technique or skill. We simply cannot afford to

rest on our laurels or gamble on our worldwide
reputation and simply wait for the market to
come to us. We stand to lose many thousands of
francs and do you know why?

VALENTINE   Yes. Because *I've* fallen in love.

CARMAREC   You're joking.

VALENTINE   Not altogether, no. Oh, my God, you've made
me forget something (*she calls out*) Ghislaine!

There is a sound of crashing glass from the kitchen.

GHISLAINE   (*Coming in*) You've just broken the soup tureen.

VALENTINE   I have? Thanks. Well, you can recover from the
shock by going out for some fresh air, round the
shops. There's money in my bag; I want fruit
and vegetables, cheese, some sort of dessert and
bread, oh, and an extra large entrecote steak
from the butchers.

GHISLAINE   (*Glancing upstairs*) Entrecote steak, Madame?
Large enough for two, I presume.

VALENTINE   Certainly for two.

GHISLAINE   (*Going out*) Quite right, Madame. That young
man upstairs will most likely eat like a horse.
Especially after . . . you know what. (*She goes
out*).

CARMAREC   May one enquire how long this grand passion of
yours has been going on?

VALENTINE   Since yesterday. It came like a flash of lightning.
A bolt from the blue.

CARMAREC   (*Confused*) Oh, ah yes, really, well, oh dear, hm.

VALENTINE   (*Smiling*) That's it. A bolt from the blue.

CARMAREC   You're chasing rainbows, Valentine.

VALENTINE   Aren't all women forever chasing rainbows?
Well, last night I caught myself a rainbow and
I'm not letting it go.

CARMAREC   What about poor old Gérard?

VALENTINE   You can forget 'poor old Gérard'. Leave him
out there in the Alps.

CARMAREC   Look, I've no wish to moralise, Valentine, but
                really, at your age ...

                CARMAREC *stops short, seeing* PATRICK *once more in
                his bath towel.* CARMAREC *stares at him, transfixed.*

VALENTINE   (*Cutting in*) If by my age you mean the age when
                the night is only for sleep, you must be living in
                the 19th Century. More than 20% of women
                today live with men younger then themselves.
                Didn't you know that? Don't you ever read
                novels or go to the theatre or read the papers?
                What makes you think I'm the wrong age to fall
                in love? Get up to date, my dear friend. I just
                happen to be in love with a man who happens to
                be twenty years younger than me, so what?
                That is of today, fashionable, à la mode.

CARMAREC   That's as may be. But I've come here about our
                perfume project and you're going to put your
                mind to it today, now.

VALENTINE   Oh not today, Carmarec, please. Today I am
                Cleopatra, Madame la Pompadour, Gloria
                Swanson, all rolled into one. And you won't
                find any of those ladies with their noses stuck in
                a scent bottle or a test tube.

CARMAREC   But, Valentine, to give up both your career *and*
                Gérard, of whom my wife and I are so fond, I
                really don't know what to say, it's ...

VALENTINE   (*Interrupting him*) It's madness, I know.

CARMAREC   But I always thought you were so happy with
                Gérard. What is this other individual like, this
                'thunderbolt from the blue'?

VALENTINE   A very different proposition. You see, Gérard
                and I were growing old together, quite
                agreeably, but I was living with a man in woolly
                combinations and bedroom slippers, you know,
                like a husband. Now, at this moment, I'm as it
                were on holiday with a young man in an
                open-necked shirt and sandals.

                At this moment the bedroom door opens and PATRICK
                appears, dressed in an open-necked shirt, to

collect his sandals from under the kitchen table. He sees
CARMAREC *and reacts violently.*

PATRICK   Oh God, oh my goodness! Oh, I beg your
           pardon. I'm awfully sorry, Sir, that our ...
           meeting should be so, well, so much of a
           confrontation.

           VALENTINE *is shaking her head at* PATRICK. *But*
           PATRICK *goes on.*

PATRICK   No, Valentine, you keep out of it. This is a
           matter between men. (*To* CARMAREC) Sir, if I'd
           known you were arriving this morning, I'd have
           prepared a more suitable explanation. The
           trouble is, I thought you were still in Geneva.

           VALENTINE *again makes a frantic signal at* PATRICK.

PATRICK   Bear with me, Sir, and I will try to act as
           diplomatically as I can. You see, Sir, Valentine
           and I ... it was like a twig falling on to the
           dying embers of a fire ... well, perhaps dying is
           not quite the right word. What I'm trying to say
           is ...

VALENTINE Don't try to say anything. This gentleman is not
           who you think he is, so shut up, will you.

PATRICK   (*Catching up*) Oh, my God, I'm so sorry, yes, I
           see ... I'd better go then. Must get to the shop.
           I'll be back for lunch, maybe a little before
           lunch, if there aren't too many deliveries to deal
           with. Excuse me. (PATRICK *makes for the door*)

VALENTINE Just a minute. Allow me to introduce Monsieur
           Carmarec, my boss, our Managing Director.
           This is Patrick. Patrick, hm, oh God, I can't
           remember your surname. (*To* CARMAREC)
           Anyway, he is Rose Petal, I mean, that's his
           flower shop. Isn't that a divine name for a
           flower shop?

PATRICK   (*Bowing*) Patrick Croisset, Sir.

CARMAREC   (*Stunned*) Aha!

VALENTINE Well, don't look so outraged, Carmarec.

CARMAREC   I'm not ... I'm ... on the contrary, I'm
           delighted, and I do hope, Monsieur Croisset,

that perhaps you will use your influence with Madame Matignon and persuade her to get down to some work for us.

CARMAREC *picks up his briefcase and puts it on the table, and a little box which he opens to bring out some bottles which he sets out in a row.*

VALENTINE   I told you, Carmarec, I can't work today. I wouldn't know how to start.

PATRICK   Of course you can. Come on, Valentine, give us a treat. Sniff, smell. Show us that famous nose of yours in action.

VALENTINE   (*Smiling*) Really?

PATRICK   (*Begging her*) Yes. Go on.

CARMAREC   (*Also pleading*) I beg you, Valentine, please, we have so little time.

VALENTINE   (*To* PATRICK) It's nothing very spectacular.

CARMAREC   (*Taking up the first bottle, to* PATRICK) Thank you, Sir.

VALENTINE   (*To* PATRICK) No smoking, if you please. Put out your cigarette.

PATRICK *puts out his cigarette.* VALENTINE *takes the first bottle from* CARMAREC, *opens it and smells it. As she opens and comments on each bottle, she strides round and round the apartment,* CARMAREC *following her, handing her the bottles in desperate anxiety.*

VALENTINE   (*Sniffing the first bottle*) You can forget that one, far too heavy, too much cassis, too much narcissus, suitable for rather stout, greedy ladies. Much too sweet and cloying. Rather revolting, really. (CARMAREC *hands her a second bottle from which she takes a little wooden dipper and puts it aside to dry and sniffs it*) Not bad. The ingredients are quite nicely blended. (*She pours some of the scent from the second bottle on to the back of her hand and smells it*) Let's see how well it clings. (*She waves her hands about*) Yes, pretty good, it diffuses well, too. (*Now she picks up the little wooden dipper and sniffs it*) Ah, yes, now that's not

bad at all. Marginally better than that one.
We'll probably need to thin out the Bergamotte
a little and add a touch more of the mandarin.
That'll bring out more the feeling of sunshine.
(VALENTINE *sniffs the back of her hand again*) No,
it's not coming through. I've got a feeling
number two, this one, has too much sediment in
it . . . not mature yet . . . needs keeping a bit.
(*Again, she sniffs the little dipper and shakes it about*)
You'd better make a note, Carmarec; this one
needs a little more mandarin and a touch more
lemon, and maybe just a teardrop of dragonfly.

CARMAREC   (*Taking the bottle and sniffing it*) You're right,
Valentine, this has a distinct flavour of sunshine.

VALENTINE   Now, let's look at number three. (VALENTINE
sniffs bottle number three, and her face screws up) Yuk!
Too much Bergamotte and far too much
Patchouli. You can pour that one straight down
the lavatory. It's revolting. (PATRICK *takes it and
smells it. Meanwhile* VALENTINE *sniffs bottle number
four*) Now for number four. Hm, I don't think I
suggested this, did I?

CARMAREC   The lab assistants were very keen to try their
own formula. They hoped it might give you a
surprise.

VALENTINE   It's a surprise alright . . . and a pretty nasty
one. The honeysuckle is far too powerful. (*She
hands it to* PATRICK, *who sniffs it with a smile*) And
the wood element is far too strong. There's even
a touch of mushroom about it. I suppose you
could market that one in Canada; make a pretty
good toilet water for lumberjacks. No, my dears,
it's got to be number two, I have no doubt
about it. Number Two is smart and chic, like
good clothes, but not too clever. It's a young
scent, vibrant and dynamic and fresh like a new
love affair.

PATRICK   A new love affair?

CARMAREC   That's it! That's what we'll call it 'Love Affair'.

VALENTINE   Wonderful ... and it diffuses well. There we
                 are, Jean, just tell them to let it settle a bit
                 longer, then bottle it, package it and let it go
                 and I'll guarantee that perfume will saturatae
                 the market on all five continents.

CARMAREC   (*Relieved*) I think I can endorse what you say.
                 yes, I agree. Grâce à Dieu!

                 CARMAREC *crosses himself with relief, then puts away
                 the other four bottles and picks up number two as
                 though it was the Precious Blood itself. Then he edges
                 up to* VALENTINE *and, to her surprise, plants a kiss on
                 her forehead.* PATRICK *also kisses her.*

PATRICK   Bravo! Valentine you're a marvel. (*To*
                 CARMAREC) Aren't we lucky, both of us, to own
                 a woman like that? Eh?

VALENTINE   Shut up and go! Take that bunch of keys from
                 the hall table.

                 PATRICK *moves towards the hall table.*

CARMAREC   Goodbye, my dear fellow and thank you for
                 your support.

PATRICK   My pleasure (PATRICK *goes out*)

CARMAREC   Valentine, my dear, I was right the first time.
                 He's a nice young man. (*Sarcastic*) Somewhat
                 long in the tooth, but pleasant enough, but
                 aren't you being just a little bit absurd?

VALENTINE   (*Laughing*) Of course I am. So absurd that I
                 can't stop laughing at myself, because I know
                 I'm being monstrously and gloriously absurd
                 ... so what?

CARMAREC   Ought you not to consider your position in
                 Paris? I mean your professional status ... you
                 have a name, you know, and a reputation.

VALENTINE   Not a name, Carmarec, just a nose.

CARMAREC   (*Gravely*) When I think of poor old Gérard
                 sweating blood out there in the Swiss Alps ...
                 (*he starts to laugh*) I'm bound to confess it makes
                 me chuckle just a little.

VALENTINE	Me, too. It was angelic of him to send me flowers but typical of his bad luck. If he'd only known, he'd have done much better to send me round a box of chocolates by the old lady in the sweet shop on the corner.
CARMAREC	Yes, if he'd ever suspected, poor man. Thank goodness my wife and I have no cause to suspect one another.
VALENTINE	Ah, now come on, Carmarec. Who are you to talk? We all know what you get up to at the perfume laboratories.
CARMAREC	What I get up to?
VALENTINE	Yes. You. I suggest you stop making love to your secretary in the bottle cupboard during the lunch hour and take the wretched girl off with you to Mont St Michel for the week.
CARMAREC	(*Bewildered and outraged*) Me ... and my secretary? Who's been spreading malicious gossip about me?
VALENTINE	Come on! They've all got your number. Go on, CARMAREC. Take her away and do it properly!
CARMAREC	(*To himself*) It's true my wife does happen to be away at the moment, skiing.
VALENTINE	And skiing instructors don't waste much time, do they?
CARMAREC	What do you mean?
VALENTINE	Go on, Carmarec! This is 1925, take your secretary away somewhere and have fun!
CARMAREC	(*Looks at* VALENTINE, *regretfully*) If I'd only known ... why, you and I might have ... well ...
VALENTINE	(*Laughing*) My dear friend, you're fifteen years too late.
	GHISLAINE *comes in now with the keys and makes for the kitchen with the shopping, swinging her hips in a sexy way.* CARMAREC *ogles her, fascinated.*
VALENTINE	(*Seeing him*) Carmarec, really, at your age! You ought to be ashamed of yourself.

CARMAREC   (*Incensed*) Me? How dare you preach to me about virtue! You of all people, the cradle-snatcher of the Champs Elysée!

> CARMAREC *picks up his bag, blows a kiss to* VALENTINE *and goes off with his head in the air.* GHISLAINE *comes in from the kitchen.*

GHISLAINE   Strip you naked, that's what they do!

VALENTINE   Who do?

GHISLAINE   Shopkeepers. Skin you, especially greengrocers. Honestly, the price of vegetables nowadays. I've put your purse back in your bag and it's almost empty.

VALENTINE   Thanks.

GHISLAINE   And the price of fruit, too. Do you know a pot of caviar's cheaper than a pineapple. So I bought a pot of caviar. And a bottle of Pernod, to wish you good luck tonight ... up there ... you know (*She nods her head towards the bedroom*) You ... and him.

VALENTINE   Are you by any chance mocking me, Ghislaine?

> GHISLAINE *sits down, opens her handbag and gets out her nail varnish, which she proceeds to apply to her nails.*

CARMAREC   Of course I'm not mocking you. You know me, I've no time for conventional behaviour. Do you think it'll last?

VALENTINE   What does it matter? Que sera sera. The important thing is to have the experience.

GHISLAINE   What was it like?

VALENTINE   Last night was fantastic! Shattering, like a movie. Rudolph Valentino rode up on a white horse in a silk mask and galloped off with me into the desert.

GHISLAINE   What did he do to you?

VALENTINE   You're much too young to be told, but I expect you can guess.

GHISLAINE   Oh, I can.

VALENTINE	I'm sure you go to the cinema sometimes and dream, don't you?
GHISLAINE	(*Laughing*) Me? Oh, yes, Madame. But my movie heroes are more down to earth characters; like the sergeant of the Foreign Legion or a lorry driver. Do you know, I have a passion for lorry drivers; they can be sympatique, but also just a little bit rough and brutal at the same time, with all that lovely engine oil on their dungarees. I dream about being roughed up a bit, you know, for someone to rip my clothes and smudge my lipstick . . . like a truck driver would . . . a man driving one of those huge lorries. All rough.
VALENTINE	Ghislaine! Stop it. Pull yourself together and cool down!
GHISLAINE	I like that coming from you! Who needs cooling down?
VALENTINE	Honestly! Your eyes were quite wild and you were almost slavering at the mouth, like a hunger striker sighting a grilled steak.
GHISLAINE	What about you, Madame?
	At this moment the door opens and PATRICK *comes in on roller skates carrying a long loaf of bread and a bottle of champagne. He skates up to and stops neatly in front of* VALENTINE. GHISLAINE *stares, amazed.* VALENTINE *smiles.* PATRICK *doesn't see* GHISLAINE, *having his back to her.*
PATRICK	Back early, darling!
VALENTINE	Allow me to introduce Ghislaine, which seems hardly necessary as she's already seen you with no clothes on! Have you suddenly grown taller or have I shrunk?
PATRICK	You've shrunk.
GHISLAINE	Well, I must push off. I'm modelling in an hour's time. Got to pose in the nude for a lot of half dead art students and they call them the life class.

VALENTINE	Ghislaine, would it be too much trouble to ask you to put the dirty dishes in the sink before you go?
GHISLAINE	But I've just done my nails.
VALENTINE	Oh, you're hopeless!
PATRICK	Don't worry, I'll wash up while Valentine gets dressed for lunch.
VALENTINE	Lunch?
PATRICK	Since you so kindly invited me to dine last night, I though I'd invite you to lunch today, here, in your apartment. Champagne, hot bread, pâté and Patrick! (PATRICK *skates off into the kitchen*) Oh, darling, yes, why not? (VALENTINE *goes off.*)
GHISLAINE	Shall I come up and help you to dress for lunch, Madame?
VALENTINE	No, but you could stay and help Monsieur Patrick in the kitchen!
GHISLAINE	Yes, of course, Madame;
PATRICK	(*Entering from the kitchen*) Now, Ghislaine. You can lay the table while I put the hot bread on ice and the Champagne in the oven. (*He goes back into the kitchen*)
GHISLAINE	Certainly, Monsieur Patrick! (GHISLAINE *starts tolay the table*) Wine glass for Monsieur Patrick, wine glass for Madame. Knife for Monsieur Patrick, knife for Madame. Fork for Monsieur Patrick ... *As* GHISLAINE *continues laying the table, the lights fade down to a blackout. Soft music is heard and* VALENTINE *appears in a pool of light. She is beautifully dressed in a new gown.*
VALENTINE	I'd quite forgotten what fun lunch can be. You see, Gérard never came here for lunch, not once in fifteen years. I'm afraid the Champagne went straight to my head, so I had to have a little lie down. Well, Patrick did too. Then he popped off to the Rose Petal. I did something really

naughty. You've guessed ... a mad shopping spree. Rather elegant isn't it? Don't ask me how much it cost! All I know is that time flies when you're having fun! Tonight it's dinner for two in a little artists' café in Montmartre. But first it's cocktails for two. I've made a wonderful new concoction. A 'Wicked Lady'.

The lights now come up on the set. Time has passed. It is evening.

PATRICK	Valentine!
VALENTINE	Patrick!
PATRICK	My darling!
VALENTINE	My darling!
PATRICK	I've missed you!
VALENTINE	It's been three whole hours!
PATRICK	The longest we've been apart.
VALENTINE	What would you say to a Wicked Lady?
PATRICK	I'd say: 'Good evening, little Wicked Lady'!
VALENTINE	To love!
PATRICK	To love! Toujours l'amour! I've got a little surprise for you.
VALENTINE	I adore surprises.

PATRICK *produces a gramophone record which he goes over to put on the gramophone and winds it up. The music of 'Yes, Sir, That's My Baby' plays on the gramophone.*

PATRICK	May I have the pleasure of this dance, Madame?
VALENTINE	Oh my God, I think I'm blushing!

PATRICK *and* VALENTINE *dance madly to the gramophone record until the telephone suddenly rings.*

VALENTINE	Oh, damn!
PATRICK	Don't answer it.
VALENTINE	I must. It might be my mother, she lives out at Versailles. Something might have happened to her. (*She picks up the telephone*).

	Hallo! Hallo! Yes! No, no! No, wait! (*She hangs up the telephone again*) Too late, he hung up.
PATRICK	Who did?
VALENTINE	Gerard did!
PATRICK	Oh. (*Pause*) What did he say?
VALENTINE	He said: 'I'm just buying some tobacco in the little cafe on the corner; be with you in a couple of minutes'.

They look at each other, horrified.

PATRICK	I forgot to tell you something.
VALENTINE	What?
PATRICK	When I got back to the shop after lunch there was another order for you from Interflora. One of the girls had made up a bouquet which I promptly threw into the dustbin.
VALENTINE	Why?
PATRICK	First, because they were from Gérard and second because they were gladioli.
VALENTINE	Gladioli? So ...
PATRICK	Gladioli are the only flowers I really hate. Not only have they no scent but they are somehow arrogant, pretentious and hostile ... sort of steel daggers. How can any man send gladioli to a woman he loves. They're the only really nasty, unpleasant blooms in existence. Don't you agree? (VALENTINE *doesn't answer*) What's the matter?
VALENTINE	He's coming and we've got to face up to it, you and I, here and now.
PATRICK	(*Laughing*) Such tragedy, my dear, such drama. Oh, no, this little scene must be played for comedy. I'll show you how to play it, shall I? (*Acting as her, to her*) Gérard, my dear, I've got a little suprise for you. No, not exactly a present. It's not even a very nice surprise, but it's all for you, and you alone. You see, the man I met while you were abroad was, on the other hand,

a very nice surprise, and I feel sure that, loving me as you do, you'll take great comfort from the fact that in your absence I have found happiness.

VALENTINE   Very funny but it won't work.

PATRICK   All right. Let's play it for melodrama. (*He goes into melodrama*) 'Gérard, my dear' (*He sinks to his knees, hands clasped together*) 'I have tragic news for you, and it's all the more tragic when I think how much this news is going to make you suffer. I'm in love with another man. Oh, I know he could never love me as you have loved me, and I wish only to act in this sad affair out of my deep deep love for you, so please, Gérard, if you love me, spurn me, leave me, for the wicked wanton woman that I am. Condemn me to my life of shame, go from me never to return.' How about that?

PATRICK *gets up again.* VALENTINE *is in fits of laughter.*

VALENTINE   I think I'd better settle for something between the two.

PATRICK   Shall I go for a walk round the block while you explain things to him? I'll give you a quarter of an hour, then come back.

VALENTINE   Come back will you? How do you know I shall want you to? How do you know I shan't burst into tears of remorse and guilt the moment I set eyes on Gérard? Doesn't it occur to you that he might forgive me and that I might fall into his arms and tell him I love him and only him, deep down in my heart; and beg him to stay with me. Aren't you afraid I might do just that?

PATRICK   No.

VALENTINE   Why not?

PATRICK   Because you know damned well that, if you did, I'd slit your throat, having first slit my own.

PATRICK *marches to the door and slams out.*
VALENTINE *smiles. After a second, the front door is opened again and* PATRICK *comes back.*

PATRICK   Correction, I should have said I'll slit your
               throat first, and *then* slit my own.

               He slams out again. VALENTINE *smiles, then seems to
               hear something. The sound of the lift coming up.
               Swiftly, she gets out a pack of cards and starts playing
               patience.* GÉRARD *enters with a suitcase and a massive
               bunch of gladioli.*

GERARD   I came straight from the station.

VALENTINE   (*Feigning surprise*) Oh, you are naughty to give
               me such a shock. (*Pause*) Did you happen to pass
               anyone on the stairs?

GERARD   No, I came up in the lift. Who should I have
               passed on the stairs?

VALENTINE   A friend of mine.

GERARD   Anyone I know?

VALENTINE   Not yet.

GERARD   (*Kissing her on both cheeks*) Ah. Well, grand to see
               you, my dear. I wanted to send you some
               flowers from Geneva, but I dared not risk the
               florist this end; so I bought you these at the
               Gare de Lyon. I hope you like gladioli, it was all
               they had left.

               VALENTINE *takes the flowers and puts them down on a
               chair.*

VALENTINE   That's not surprising.

GERARD   Why?

VALENTINE   Because florists find gladioli very difficult flowers
               to get rid of.

GERARD   How do you mean, get rid of?

VALENTINE   Oh, for God's sake, because they are far too
               bulky to carry about; much too big.

GERARD   Ah, yes, that's right. Most people live in very
               small flats these days don't they, with very small
               flower vases. Is that what you mean?

VALENTINE   (*Stuffing the gladioli into a vase*) There we are,
               gladioli (*She sniffs them*) which, oddly enough,
               give off a subtle aura of sandalwood. (*A pause*)

GERARD	You seem a little on edge, my dear. Are you?
VALENTINE	I've been a little on edge for nigh on 15 years, Gérard.

GERARD *opens his suitcase and starts to hang his clothes in a cupboard.*

GERARD	That's just as well. Mustn't get too complacent, must we?
VALENTINE	(*Smelling his clothes as he unpacks them*) Mmm. Amber tinged with sandalwood. And, how about you?
GERARD	How about me, what?
VALENTINE	You're not on edge, I suppose.
GERARD	I say, be a good girl and pour me a drink will you?
VALENTINE	(*Still sniffing*) Chypre and a little rose and pear with just a touch of Quarantaine.
GERARD	What's that you said about quarantine?
VALENTINE	Nothing, I was just describing a plant of the Wattiole family, highly scented and rather rare in France. Whisky?
GERARD	You know perfectly well I don't drink whisky; haven't you got anything else? Some of that Muscadet?
VALENTINE	Sorry, I've drunk it all.
GERARD	Pity; ah well, tell me your news.
VALENTINE	(*Taking the plunge*) Gérard, there's something you've got to know.
GERARD	What?

VALENTINE *changes her mind.*

VALENTINE	Ghislaine hasn't done out our room.
GERARD	That doesn't matter. What I want to know is what have you been up to while I've been away?
VALENTINE	I was going to ask you the same question. How did the job go?
GERARD	Very well. What is it Valentine? You seem almost relieved that I'm a day late. I thought

perhaps not getting here yesterday, I might as
well come on the Wednesday instead. Isn't that
alright?

VALENTINE   There was no need to come today. It wasn't
your fault your work delayed you. What was the
weather like in Switzerland?

GERARD   Excellent. What's it been like here?

VALENTINE   Quite honestly, I wouldn't know, I've hardly
put my nose out of doors.

GERARD   Oh, you haven't been to work then?

VALENTINE   No.

GERARD   (*Surprised*) Well, well! (*A pause*) Overtired, I
expect. That perfume place is too much for you.
I've always said so. It'll destroy your health and
age you before your time.

VALENTINE   Will it? Well I feel 20 today and fit as a fiddle.

GERARD   You may say so, but I know you pretty well and
. . .

VALENTINE   (*Angry*) Gérard, If you've only come here to
make a lot of idiotic remarks, you can either go
straight to Geneva and stay there or, if you must
come, wait for another Tuesday sometime next
year. (*Sniffing*) Cloves, but more jasmine, yes,
quite a strong element of jasmine.

GERARD   You are in a state, aren't you?

VALENTINE   I'm not in the least bit of state; I'm perfectly
calm.

GERARD   Oh, I say, you'll never guess what caused my
delay. An Emir.

VALENTINE   A what?

GERARD   Arab fellow. Sheikh of some sort. Wanted a
full-sized Turkish bath and a private mosque in
his garden; and quite willing to pay for it. That
was a nightmare. Had to give in to him of
course but only for the Turkish bath. It was
endless discussions with the carpet people that
finally made me miss my connection. Do you
want me to tell you about it?

VALENTINE	No. I am not remotely interested in your Emir, and I do not wish to hear another word about your adventures in Switzerland. Do you understand? Not another word.
GERARD	Oh, yes you do. I can read you like a book.
VALENTINE	Read me, can you? In that case, you need a new pair of spectacles.
GERARD	I don't need spectacles to see that you are being exceedingly disagreeable and distant.
VALENTINE	Really? Well, I can read you like a book too, and what I read very clearly is a woman in the offing.
GERARD	You're crazy.
VALENTINE	I'm telling you straight, Gérard, I can smell a chic female. (*She sniffs him*) Not an Arab Sheikh. That's Lily of the Valley, that means a young woman and sandalwood, that signifies an oriental, (*She sniffs again*) a strong element of clover and lotus flower, that's Egyptian. There's an Egyptian girl in your life, isn't there? Well?
GERARD	(*Shrugging his shoulders*) I told you, I've been dealing with an Emir. What you can smell is elderly Arab.

VALENTINE *takes from his jacket a handerchief covered in lipstick and holds it up to* GÉRARD.

VALENTINE	Who wears lipstick?
GERARD	Oh, my God, how can anyone live with a woman with a nose, Valentine, it's perfectly simple . . . (*From now on* GÉRARD *starts to twist and turn and say anything that comes into his head*).
GERARD	Absolutely simple to explain. While I was lunching in the Wagon Restaurant of the train from Geneva, we went rather fast over some points. The whole train sort of bumped and swerved and a girl on the way to her table sort of fell into my lap. She had a slight cold, so I lent her my clean pocket handkerchief to blow her . . .

VALENTINE *has now found a piece of paper in*
GÉRARD's *suit pocket.*

VALENTINE   What's this bill? Hotel de la Montagne, Geneva.
             Suite for two persons with double bed. Extra
             Charges. Dinner en suite, caviar and
             champagne. 3200 francs?

GERARD   (*Improvising*) It was an accident. The lift in the
             hotel broke down. She was very scared, this little
             girl, so she clung on to me in the dark, because
             the light went out; she was Egyptian, the girl
             was, rather small with almond eyes, little dark
             almond eyes. And scared. (VALENTINE *laughs*)
             What's so funny about that?

VALENTINE   Its not funny. Its really terribly sad. As soon as
             a man goes off on a business trip, you merely
             wait for him to come back and tell you a whole
             pack of lies; like going to Geneva ostensibly to
             build chalets, but really in pursuit of a young
             girl, a child … honestly, at your age. Aren't
             you ashamed of yourself?

GERARD   You're making a mountain out of a molehill;
             there was nothing to it.

VALENTINE   (*Becoming shrill*) What do you mean, nothing to
             it. You make me sick. How dare you lie to me?
             Me, who's been faithful to you and stuck to you
             for 15 years like a slave. Yes, a young slave who
             sacrificed the best years of her life to look after
             you and nurse you through your rheumatic fever
             and your chest colds. An unpaid hospital nurse,
             that's what I've been.

GERARD   That's hysterical nonsense, Valentine. You're
             not yourself today.

VALENTINE   Not myself? Oh, I see, so its me whose behaving
             abnormally, isn't it? I, whose only desire has
             been to live for you and wait on you like a vestal
             virgin, or rather like a mother. Do you realise
             how many times I could have taken off and
             deserted you?

GERARD   Valèntine, Valentine. Come on, there's
           something the matter. What is it? We know
           each other well enough, surely.

VALENTINE No, we don't! We don't know each other at all.
           I've no intention of staying any longer with an
           ageing lecher who goes about deflowering little
           Egyptian girls in lifts.

GERARD   That's rubbish. She is not a little girl; she's 33.
           And it didn't happen in the lift.

VALENTINE 33, there you are, you've admitted it. You're a
           dirty old man. I'm not sure which of you is the
           more disgusting, you or her. On balance, I
           think you are. Quite disgusting! Carrying on
           like that without a single thought for me. Me,
           sitting here in Paris, thinking of nothing but
           you, wondering how you were, and waiting to
           welcome you back with a delicious dinner of
           Cold Beef in Aspic, which I may say was a
           nightmare to prepare, and quite excellent it was
           too. Oh, I'm just a stupid fool, a mug, an idiot.
           (*She looks at the bedroom door and realises the absurdity
           of her outburst*) No. Luckily, I'm not a complete
           idiot, not at all. (*She is calm now*) How old did
           you say this girl was?

GERARD   33.

VALENTINE Well, well. Its rather splendid really; my dear
           old lover has finally managed to seduce a slinky,
           sexy little faun with firm breasts, a sun-tanned
           body and eyes of jade. Then, clutching his
           suitcase in one sweaty little hand and a dozen
           gladioli in the other, back he comes to my
           apartment with his little head bowed in shame,
           to find me exactly where he left me, quite alone.
           But darling, why didn't you offer yourself to her
           every night for a whole week and really put her
           under your magic spell?

           GERARD *remains some way from her and motionless.*

VALENTINE No, don't touch me. Never try to touch me
           again, Gérard, never.

> VALENTINE *goes off into her room.* GÉRARD *remains
> alone in the living room with his head indicating that
> she is rather over-playing her hand. Then he spots a
> pair of roller skates in a corner of the room on a table
> with a note attached to them. He examines the skates
> and reads the note. Then, hearing* VALENTINE
> *returning, he sits down quickly to continue reading the
> paper nonchalanntly.* VALENTINE *comes in again.*

VALENTINE   Do you fancy a little slice of cold beef?

GERARD   (*Sharply*) No, I don't. I'm not hungry.

VALENTINE   I must say you look frightfully well; probably
the moutain air;

GERARD   Probably.

VALENTINE   Darling, I have a confession to make.

GERARD   Ghislaine *has* done our room.

VALENTINE   (*Thrown*) No, it's a ... I'm well ... rather at
sixes and sevens. I suppose its being Wednesday
today and not Tuesday, with Ghislaine not here,
except that she has been here after all. Everyone
seems to have been here today. It's all kind of
got me in a muddle.

GERARD   Would you rather I went home?

VALENTINE   Would you rather go?

GERARD   No, I wouldn't, but would you? (*Reading from the
newspaper he has just picked up*) Marseilles widow of
50 found decapitated; former gigolo of 30 faces
charges. That's the stuff to make you think.

A slight Pause.

VALENTINE   (*Looks resolved and then addresses* GÉRARD, *who still
sits in a chair*) Gérard, relax will you, dear, and
put your feet up, because sooner of later you've
got to be told that ... (*She stops herself*).

GERARD   Told what, sooner or later?

VALENTINE   I'm trying to say that, sooner or later, you're
always very welcome here in my flat. Any time.
That goes without saying.

GERARD	Even on a Wednesday?
VALENTINE	Even on a Wednesday. As for your little extravaganza in Geneva, I shall put that down to the warm weather.
GERARD	That's very generous of you, my dear; very sporting, typically tolerant, if I may say so, and very much in your style.

VALENTINE *goes off to the kitchen with a slight grin.*

GERARD	(*As she goes*) Don't overdo it, old boy. (GÉRARD *sits on the sofa again*) Do you now, I read quite an interesting article coming back in the train, all about this new craze for roller skating. Do you think *I* ought to take it up?
VALENTINE	(*Returning from the kitchen*) If it's the latest craze, I advise you to ignore it.
GERARD	By the way, you still haven't told me what you got up to while I was away.
VALENTINE	Me? Oh, nothing very interesting. Just the usual routine life of a research chemist. You know, travelling to and from the laboratories, discussing matters with Carmarec.
GERARD	You told me you hadn't been to the laboratories.
VALENTINE	(*Caught out*) Did I? Oh, how extraordinary.

GERARD *gets up and goes over to lift the lid of the gramophone.*

GERARD	Let's have some music, shall we?
VALENTINE	Must we?
GERARD	(*Picks up the record and looks at it*) 'Yes Sir, That's My Baby'. Hm, that's a new one, isn't it? Someone give it to you?
VALENTINE	Yes.
GERARD	Been dancing to it, have you?
VALENTINE	Yes.
GERARD	With a man?

VALENTINE	Naturally.
	A pause.
GERARD	(*Brandishing the skates and note*) With Patrick, no doubt.
VALENTINE	That's private.
GERARD	(*Reading the note*) Darling, I've had your roller skates mended for you. If I'm not there, I'll be in my bedroom or in the bath. Come up, I love you, Patrick. Your 'V'.
	A long silence.
VALENTINE	Oh, well. Its a relief in a way. Now I really have nothing to say to you. There is . . . nothing I can say.
GERARD	(*Looking at her*) You've been naughty, haven't you? Admit it.
VALENTINE	I haven't been naughty Gérard. I've committed an act of total madness. It's nothing tangible that you can actually see. I'm being blown away by the wind, up through the damp clouds and into the sun, where I feel all warm and wonderful.
GERARD	I see. Well, you can fold your wings now and come down to earth. You've been extremely wicked and you have the nerve to criticise me. How dare you?
VALENTINE	Ah, well. You see my experience has been quite abstract, a sort of sacred mission, to prove something.
GERARD	Are you trying to pull my leg?
VALENTINE	Not really. Well, yes, I suppose I am. It's middle-aged men. They look in the mirror at their greying temples and think themselves irresistable. All right, so why shouldn't a woman of 50, provided her face isn't too lined and her hair reasonably tidy, also believe herself to be irresistible?
GERARD	Valentine, you have slept around in my absence and you intend to go on sleeping with him.

That's no passing fancy, that's organised
adultery and I find it quite disgusting.

VALENTINE   Now look, to start with you and I are not
            married. So there can be no question of
            adultery. So there's nothing disgusting about it.
            On the contrary it was a Christian act. I
            assumed the cloak of Saint Martin, who taught
            us to share ourselves with others. Its politically
            and socially desirable and economically too,
            because it helps defeat inflation. What used to
            divide into two, can now be divided into three.
            Shared between three people. So that's that.

GERARD   You are sleeping with another person.

VALENTINE   That's right. Another man. But not one below
            the age of puberty.

GERARD   At 33? Have you been drinking? Is that why all
            the Muscadet is gone?

VALENTINE   I'm completely sober, Gérard.

GERARD   All right. What about this person, are you in
            love with him?

VALENTINE   I don't know about being in love with him, all I
            know is I'm crazy about him.

GERARD   And he's crazy about you?

VALENTINE   That's the impression he gives me.

GERARD   And how long has this been going on?

VALENTINE   Since yesterday.

GERARD   Its monstrous.

VALENTINE   Its not monstrous. It's wonderful. And what's
            more it's your fault. You sent him to me, you
            did. And you must forgive me, because in all
            the excitement, I've completely forgotten to
            thank you for him.

GERARD   (*Dazed*) I don't understand.

VALENTINE   You sent me flowers, didn't you?

GERARD   I did.

VALENTINE   Well, you sent me a florist as well.

GERARD	I sent you a florist?
VALENTINE	Veni, Vidi, Vici. When you sent me flowers through Interflora, the florist came with them. The florist saw me, and the florist conquered me.
GERARD	How ridiculous!
VALENTINE	Not really. You see, we have quite a lot in common, me and my florist. We are both interested in scent.
GERARD	Is he younger them me?
VALENTINE	Let me look at you. Yes, I suppose a bit.
GERARD	There you are, you see. Well, all I can say is I'm finished Valentine, shattered, and speechless.
VALENTINE	So you should be. Its either remorse for what you've done to me, or guilt for abandoning that unfortunate Egyptian girl in Geneva.
GERARD	That's what you think. I have news for you, dearest. She's not in Geneva now, she's in Paris, staying at the Ritz.
VALENTINE	Oh! Followed you to Paris has she?
GERARD	We happened to be on the same train, purely by chance. As a matter of fact, we parted at the station flower stall. *She* chose the gladioli for you.
VALENTINE	(*Dryly*) I know, I can tell by their smell.
GERARD	The whole thing for me was one insane passionate holocaust of fire.
VALENTINE	Whose embers are now cooling off at the Ritz. Don't tell me you're not going to try and rekindle that little fire.
GERARD	Don't tell me you're not jealous!
VALENTINE	Jealous? Oh, no! Much worse that that! I'm heartbroken.
GERARD	Oh, for God's sake, I told you, we parted at the Gare de Lyon.

VALENTINE	And what did you say to each other when you parted?
GERARD	We said 'au revoir', that's all.
VALENTINE	(*Triumphant*) There you are, you see.
GERARD	What do I see?
VALENTINE	'Au revoir', 'til we meet again. You intend to see her again, don't you.
GERARD	Look, I don't think I can take much more of this ...

The key turns in the lock. PATRICK *comes in with a grin on his face. All three stand rigidly looking at each other.*

VALENTINE	(*Dead calm*) Do you know something? I had such an odd dream last night. All through the dream you two were chasing after each other but never quite managing to meet. Well, now that I'm awake and you've finally caught up with each other, allow me to introduce you. Patrick, this is Gérard. Gérard, this is Patrick. I won't recite your life stories to each other, because you've both heard them from me. (*A silence*)
VALENTINE	Alright. Now we must come to a decision, mustn't we? And how shall we reach it? Standing up? Sitting down? With a glass of wine in our hands? With a little toast? I'm afraid I lied to you, Gérard, there *is* some white wine in the fridge ... would you care for a glass?

PATRICK *grins.* GÉRARD *is obviously very put out by this embarrassing scene.*

VALENTINE	I read once, when I was young, a book I found in my mother's room, written by a Lady somebody or other, I can't remember her name. There was a chapter in it entitled 'Advice To A Woman Of The World Who Happens To Have A Husband And The Good Fortune To Possess Several Lovers As Well'. I can't remember what the advice was now ... pity. (*A pause*) Ah, well. You two can do as you please. Personally, I'm going to sit down.

VALENTINE *sits down.* PATRICK *likewise.* GÉRARD
remains on his feet, bewildered.

GERARD   (*Coming out of a dream*) That's not him is it?

VALENTINE   Certainly, that's him.

PATRICK   That's right, it's me. (*To* VALENTINE, *indicating*
              GÉRARD) Are you sure that's him this time?

GERARD   It's not him. You're pulling my leg. It doesn't
              make sense.

VALENTINE   (*Sarcastic*) No, of course not, you're quite right. I
              hired him from one of those catering firms who
              provide waiters for cocktail parties, just to pay
              you back for your Egyptian friend.

              GÉRARD *comes to* VALENTINE, *bends over her and
              looks into her eyes.*

GERARD   Look at me, straight in the eye.

VALENTINE   I am looking at you, and do you know what I
              can see? I can see total incomprehension and
              bewilderment. Yours are the eyes of an outraged
              male, who is saying to himself 'it's perfectly
              normal for a man of over 50 to seduce a young
              girl. It is, on the other hand, quite unnatural
              and unthinkable, for a woman in her 50's to
              seduce a young man. I don't know what you are
              reading in my eyes, Gérard dear, but I can read
              yours very, very, clearly.

GERARD   (*Shattered*) I don't know what to say, I just don't.
              When I look at this young chap . . .

VALENTINE   And then look at me. Yes, we know what you're
              thinking, thank you very much.

GERARD   I simply don't know what to say. I can't find the
              right words to . . .

PATRICK   Then let's play a little word game, and see if we
              can find some for you. How about unrepentant?

VALENTINE   Or unbearable. Unacceptable.

GERARD   Now look here, this is no time for games, the
              matter is too serious.

PATRICK   Serious? She won't take it seriously, there's no
                 point in trying to make her. That's where you
                 go wrong with Valentine. Poor old Gérard, your
                 emotions are churning around inside you like a
                 cement mixer, you've become a sort of concrete
                 block.

GERARD   Its better than being a rolling stone!

VALENTINE   (*Interrupting*) Come on now, that's enough. I've
                 been having a good think, and I've come to the
                 conclusion, in the course of my good think, that
                 I need to be left alone. I want to ponder things a
                 little longer. So you can, both of you, be
                 angelic, and depart to your respective abodes.
                 Go on! Out of it, the pair of you.

                 The two men take a stop forward in protest.

VALENTINE   No, I mean it. If you want to please me, that's
                 what you can both do.

PATRICK   (*Furious*) What? Go now, at this vital moment?

GERARD   Valentine, please!

VALENTINE   I'll telephone you both, I promise. Later on.

PATRICK   You mean we shall be summoned here and told
                 which of us you prefer? Which makes your heart
                 stand still? Which arouses you physically? Or
                 shall we, all three of us, remain in a sort of
                 tripartite embrace, until you make up your
                 mind.

VALENTINE   Don't be absurd.

GERARD   Now, listen, Valentine. I've got something
                 serious to say to you, something we've talked
                 about before. Supposing we got married, you
                 and I . . .

VALENTINE   Oh, God. (*She starts to laugh*) What a dreadful
                 thing to suggest. It's bad enough to be a boring
                 old couple for three nights a week, but *every*
                 night of the week, I can think of nothing worse.

GERARD   Be sensible, Valentine, after all at our age . . .

VALENTINE   Our age? Your age, if you like, not my. Do you
              realise that in the last 24 hours I've shed 24
              years? I'm surprised you haven't noticed.

PATRICK   (*Imitating* GÉRARD) Now listen, Valentine. I've
              got something serious to say to you. If you and I
              were to get married instead of ...

              VALENTINE *Bursts out laughing.*

VALENTINE   There you are, you see, he's mad, a fool, and
              clown, and he makes me laugh. Oh, do take
              that funereal expression off your face Gérard or
              I shall burst into tears. Go home, both of you,
              and get some sleep. I'll let you know what I
              decide, I promise. Just leave me alone.

              The two men go out.

VALENTINE   (*To herself*) How odd that Gérard and I both
              happened to ... needed to have a little fling at
              exactly the same moment, although we were
              hundreds of miles apart. There must have been
              something special in the air the last few days. I
              suppose an astrologer would say that Venus was
              passing too close to some naughty little planet in
              the firmament. (*She sits down*) Oh, how important
              it is to feel young. If I didn't catch my breath a
              little every now and then, my heart would break
              down and every other part of my body. I feel as
              though I've been swept for several miles by a
              tidal wave. Now, after all that buffeting on the
              ocean waves, a little peace and solitude, at last.

              *She stretches out on the chaise longue luxuriantly. At
              this point a key grates in the lock, the door opens and a
              young man with a suitcase walks in.* VALENTINE *sees
              him, cries out with joy, gets up off the chaise longue,
              and runs to embrace him.*

VALENTINE   Jerome, darling!

              BLACKOUT.

              CURTAIN.

Act II

Scene One

The next morning. Remains of breakfast on the table, coffee pot, etc. JEROME *is sitting at the table, dressed in his pyjamas, drinking coffee.* VALENTINE *comes in, wearing a housecoat. She pauses and strokes his head, kissing him fondly.*

VALENTINE Good morning darling. How did you sleep? (JEROME *nods*) Good! Now you must tell your mother all your news. I didn't want to grill you last night, when you were obviously tired from a long sea voyage, but I *have* got lots of questions to ask you. Why, for instance, didn't you warn me you were coming? Was there an earthquake out there in the Caribbean? I mean, I have been begging you for the last six years to try and spend your leave here with me, and you've always found some excuse not to come. And you only write to me once in a blue moon.

JEROME (*Interrupting her*) I've told you, mama, its almost impossible to get away from the plantation. There's so much to do all the year round. As to writing letters ... well, you know what a nightmare its always been for me. I hate writing letters.

VALENTINE So what is the reason for your rather sudden, unheralded arrival in Paris, all the way from the Caribbean?

JEROME A woman.

VALENTINE A woman? How interesting. Does she live in Paris?

JEROME No, she lives out there in La Marie Galante, where I work, and I'm going to marry her.

VALENTINE So, I'm to be a grandmother at last! How splendid. (*Half to herself*) Not quite the moment I'd have chosen for that, but never mind. (*Out loud*) I'm sure I shall adore my little daughter-in-law. Have you a snapshot to show me?

JEROME	No need, she's here.
VALENTINE	Where?
JEROME	In Paris. At an hotel, with her mother. We all came over together.
VALENTINE	Oh, I see. Tell me something, just so that I don't get too much of a shock when I meet them. Are these ladies from the Caribbean black or white?
JEROME	White. I thought you ought to meet them, so I've arranged for us all to have tea at the Ritz at half past three.
VALENTINE	How lovely. What's the daughter's name?
JEROME	Cherry. Cherry Montillier.
VALENTINE	(*Dryly*) What a sweet name.
JEROME	The Montillier plantation is a very good one, sugar cane and masses of it. Very profitable. We want to try and persuade you to come out there for the wedding.
VALENTINE	Perhaps I shall. (*She moves towards the bedroom*) I must say I can't wait to meet Cherry. I've just got to iron a dress, so be a darling, and put your breakfast things in the sink, will you? I'll wash them up later.

VALENTINE *goes off to her bedroom.* JEROME *finishes his coffee, gets up, and is about to take the breakfast things to the kitchen, when* GHISLAINE *comes in. She calls out.*

GHISLAINE	(*Not seeing* JEROME) Hullo! Are you there? I was just passing, so I've brought back your keys. Thought you might need them, so ... (GHISLAINE *now catches sight of* JEROME *in his pyjamas, breakfast pots in his hand. He stares at her, rooted to the spot. To herself*) My God, not another.
JEROME	(*Smiling*) Good morning.
GHISLAINE	(*Dazed*) This *is* Madame Matignon's apartment?
JEROME	Yes, that's right. She is ironing a dress. Do you want her?

GHISLAINE   (*Weak, Gulping*) What?

JEROME   I said 'Do you want to see Madame Matignon?'

GHISLAINE   Oh! Why? No! I mean ... is she alright?

JEROME   Perfectly alright.

GHISLAINE   I see. Well, that's all right then. Just as well
             she's in, because I've taken the liberty of
             bringing back her keys because, well, could you
             tell her they're here. It's her maid. (GHISLAINE
             *puts the keys down on the table. Looking meaningfully
             at* JEROME) No doubt she'll be wanting yet
             another set of keys cut for this madhouse.
             (GHISLAINE *moves to the door*)

JEROME   Are you going?

GHISLAINE   Yes. I've got to pose naked for my fellow
             students at the Art School. Please wish Madame
             Matignon luck from me in her latest adventure,
             and tell her I look forward to seeing her descend
             the grand staircase at the Folies Bérgère, flanked
             by *all* her beautiful boys.

             GHISLAINE *goes out of the flat. After a moment,*
             VALENTINE *comes out from her bedroom, dressed.*

VALENTINE   Who was that?

JEROME   A maid of some sort. Rather a talkative one, she
             jabbered away like a parrot, apparently she is off
             to pose in the nude for some students. Funny
             thing for a maid to do. Anyway, she left you a
             bunch of keys, wishes you luck and success, and
             went. Frankly, I don't understand.

VALENTINE   Don't worry darling. Go up and have your
             bath.

             JEROME *goes out.* VALENTINE *starts tidying up the
             room, then the bell rings.* VALENTINE *a bit puzzled,
             goes to open the door to a woman of about her own age,
             rather smartly dressed, in a hat with veil, gloves, etc.
             This is* BRIGITTE MONTILLIER.

BRIGITTE   Madame Matignon?

             VALENTINE *nods.*

BRIGITTE	Brigitte Montillier. I don't suppose your son has had time to tell you the news.
VALENTINE	Oh, yes he has, and I'm delighted to meet you. Please come in and sit down. To be quite honest, I thought we were going to meet later on at tea time. However, breakfast time is just as good, isn't it? May I offer you some coffee?
BRIGITTE	No thank you. To tell you the truth, I'm rather nervous.
VALENTINE	Really? Jerome's just about getting into his bath, but he did mention the engagement. What splendid news. Really quite romantic. I gather your sugar plantation is a very fine one?
BRIGITTE	Yes. It's still in my mother's name, but it will come to me eventually.
VALENTINE	(*Surprised*) Your mother? Still . . . is she? Well, of course, I know the climate in the Caribbean is very healthy, people tend to live a long time out there, don't they? I wouldn't mind going there myself, for a bit of rejuvenation.
BRIGITTE	My poor mother is dreadfully tired, after such a long journey.
VALENTINE	Oh, I see. You brought her as well.
BRIGITTE	She's dying to meet you.
VALENTINE	I shall be delighted to meet her. Poor old lady, upset by the voyage. Well, I'm afraid weddings don't make grannies feel any younger, or mummies for that matter. Don't you agree?
BRIGITTE	You look very young, Madame, if I may say so. I was quite surprised when I came in just now.
VALENTINE	So was I when I saw you. You are also very young looking, if I may say so. You and I are both of an age, Madame, when we have to take good care of our looks, don't we? Backs to the wall, warding off the arch enemy, age. It's the last battle for us. 15, 20 years, then comes the surrender, our final surrender. But we must talk about more cheerful things. Let's talk about the

young ones. I'm dying to meet your dear
mother, but even more anxious to meet my
future daughter-in-law. Tell, me, is she like
you?

BRIGITTE   I don't quite understand.

VALENTINE   I said, I can't wait to meet Cherry.

BRIGITTE   (*Puzzled*) But I'm Cherry.

VALENTINE   I beg your pardon? Oh God, oh no . . .

              VALENTINE *reels from the shock but then recovers.*

BRIGITTE   Oh, but you *must* call me Cherry.

VALENTINE   Alright, Cherry, then. But I'd rather, if you
              don't mind, that you didn't address me as
              Mother-in-Law. Incidentally, don't you think
              'Brigitte' is a slightly more appropriate name for
              a woman of your . . . build?

BRIGITTE   That's what I keep telling Jerome, but he will
              insist on calling me Cherry. You see, it was his
              idea. It dates from our first, well, the first time
              we . . . if you understand what I'm trying to
              say.

VALENTINE   Oh, I understand alright. I can see it all *too*
              clearly. The heat, the mangrove swamps, the
              mosquitoes, that intoxicating wine made from
              beetroot, the hammock at siesta time, a single
              woman out there in that foetid atmosphere. Oh,
              yes, I know the scene. I've read books about
              that sort of thing. And tell me, Cherry dear,
              when exactly did my son succumb and seduce
              you?

BRIGITTE   Oh, your son didn't seduce me.

VALENTINE   Well, he may not have started things, but I
              mean . . . when?

BRIGITTE   It happened for the first time just six years ago,
              and it *was* the first time, literally, for me.

              VALENTINE *stares at her amazed.*

VALENTINE   Six years ago? But Jerome was a child six years
              ago! My little boy, my darling, I suppose he

couldn't help himself out there in that steamy, torrid climate. So it happened ... how ... where ...?

BRIGITTE   Down among the sugar cane, Madame, and that after 18 months of hesitation, uncertainty and inner conflict. It was my education and religious principles that held me back.

VALENTINE   You held back for 18 months? What courage! And what an example to us all. Congratulations.

BRIGITTE   Mind you, Jerome held back longer than I did.

VALENTINE   That I can understand. I must say it all seems to have been a bit slow and sluggish, your passion, like with his father. Are you sure it's not going to be embarrassing for you and give you a dreadful complex to share your life with my fine, young, strapping son?

BRIGITTE   Not at all. I've convinced myself, once and for all, that I'm younger than he is. Do you know, I actually believe it.

VALENTINE   Well, I'm damned. That would never have occurred to me. You've really opened my eyes.

BRIGITTE   Of course, we've been living in sin, but I was quite happy to. Then, suddenly, a month ago, Jerome asked me to marry him. Now for the last few weeks he's been terribly impatient with me because from the moment he proposed to me we've become almost like strangers, hardly speaking to each other.

VALENTINE   In Heaven's name, why not?

BRIGITTE   Because I want to be married in white, you see, like a young bride. I believe in it. Not only for mother's sake, but for my own inner peace of mind.

VALENTINE   Yes, well I suppose a white wedding dress is always flattering, sort of rejuvenating. The only thing is ...

BRIGITTE   (*Interrupting*) Oh, I know what's bothering you.

VALENTINE   Do you?

BRIGITTE	Yes, it's the rather noticeable difference ...
VALENTINE	In your heights?
BRIGITTE	In our financial standing. After all, I am a wealthy heiress, and Jerome is a young man without prospects or expectations. He's on the make, isn't he?
VALENTINE	I'm afraid I find that remark offensive.
BRIGITTE	Oh, I'm not criticising him, I love him as he is.
VALENTINE	And you have absolutely no qualms about the difference in your ages? Not afraid of ridicule? Ah, well, I suppose down there in the mangrove swamps there's nobody to gossip about you, except a few tigers and ostriches.
BRIGITTE	As we say in La Marie Galante 'Ouche Outon Yani Ti Pousse Pousse'.
VALENTINE	Oh, I'm sure you're right. (*To herself*) Yani Ti Pousse Pousse. (*Out loud*) All the same, Cherry, just think, in 10, 20 years' time ...
BRIGITTE	20 rich years we shall have had by then and soon we shall begin to move almost imperceptibly away from wild passion towards gentle love and from gentle love into warm tenderness. You see, one has to take life as ...
VALENTINE	Yes and there, I *must* stop you because I do know the rest of it by heart. Well, Cherry, I cannot do other than wish you luck. I would go as far as to say that I can almost see the finger of Almighty God in this particular pie, and that finger tells me ... (*She makes a scolding gesture with her finger*) But that's another matter. Would you like me to fetch your fiancée, if he's ready?
BRIGITTE	(*Getting up*) No, no, just tell him to collect me from the hotel. We're off to the cemetery in Montmartre. Mother wants to look up some of our family's tombstones.
VALENTINE	I suppose that's one way of enjoying 'Gay Paree'.
BRIGITTE	May I kiss you, Madame?

The two women embrace.

VALENTINE	All I beg of you is to insist that next time you and my son have a good old tumble in the mangrove swamps, he names you after a more suitable fruit ... like a melon or a pineapple.
BRIGITTE	Oh, he never would. You see, it was he who declared that I had lips like cherries. (BRIGITTE *goes out*)
VALENTINE	(*Eyes to heaven*) Oh, he did, did he? (*The door is heard to close*) 'We shall move imperceptibly from wild passion to gentle love and from gentle love to tenderness'. I like that. (PATRICK *comes in*) And talk of the devil, here is the object of *my* tenderness.
PATRICK	Is the coast clear? And who the hell was that?
VALENTINE	Far too long to explain and you're not supposed to be here.
PATRICK	I wanted to ask you what you were planning to do for Easter.
VALENTINE	Easter? That's weeks ahead.
PATRICK	You've got to book early for Easter. Hotels and things. I thought we might go skiing.
VALENTINE	Skiing is hardly a dignified or graceful occupation for a mature woman of the world.
PATRICK	I'll be alongside you to look after you. You only need slither gently down the nursery slopes.
VALENTINE	And end up on my bum in a snowdrift.
PATRICK	Well, whatever we do, please let's spend Easter together.

JEROME, *now naked to the waist, opens the bathroom door and appears. He calls out.*

JEROME	Darling, what have you done with my toothpaste?
VALENTINE	On the bathroom shelf, darling.

JEROME *goes back into the bathroom and closes the door.* PATRICK *looks stunned.*

VALENTINE   Alright, Patrick, I know what you're thinking. The fact is that last night something very strange occurred. I was lying there on my own . . .

But PATRICK *has already stormed out, slamming the door behind him.*

VALENTINE   (*To herself, delighted*) Now who's jealous?

JEROME *crosses the room and calls.*

JEROME   Has that chap gone already? Who was he?

VALENTINE   A friend. (*She forces a smile*) Darling, I've just met Cherry.

JEROME   Good Lord! Do you mean to say she came here by herself?

VALENTINE   That's right. All by her little self. I think she's old enough by now to cross the street without someone holding her hand.

JEROME *now comes into the living room, putting on his dressing gown.*

JEROME   Yes, I suppose so. Pity. I wanted it to be a surprise.

VALENTINE   Oh, it was a surprise alright, believe me. Now, tell me, darling, truthfully, what is it about Cherry that attracts you so much?

JEROME   She has fine qualities and it's a fine plantation.

VALENTINE   Yes, I can see the attraction of *that*.

JEROME   Tell me what you think, seriously.

VALENTINE   Me? I think she's charming. You won't have many children but I'm sure she'll make you very happy.

JEROME   Now, you tell me something. Who was that friend of yours, who slammed out just now as soon as he saw me?

VALENTINE   As I said, a friend, who just happened to drift into my life and it's thanks to him, really, that I'm pleased that Cherry has drifted into yours.

JEROME   I suppose you've dropped that architect chap, have you?

VALENTINE	Not exactly.
JEROME	You're a very wicked woman, do you know that?
VALENTINE	Darling, darling. You must realise that your poor mother, as she grows older, desperately needs company more and more and it is just a little bit your fault, my ever absent son, that I find myself in this rather delicious dilemma.
JEROME	I suppose you're right, mama, yes you are, absolutely right. I agree. I've neglected you and I'm sorry.

He sits on his mother's knee and cuddles her. At this moment, PATRICK *comes in again, followed by* GÉRARD.

PATRICK	(*Indicating the scene*) There you are, now you see why she wanted to be alone. Didn't I tell you?
VALENTINE	(*Laughing*) Let me introduce you both to my splendid son, Jerome.

Immediately, both the men become warmly affectionate.

GERARD	(*To* JEROME) Jerome! I can't believe it. How you've grown and you've cut your hair shorter. Well done, old boy!
PATRICK	Greetings, Jerome.
VALENTINE	He came to introduce me to his fiancée, she's called Cherry.
PATRICK	Cherry? That ... in the hat .. and ... Well, there you are! (*To* VALENTINE) Who's cradle-snatching now!
VALENTINE	Exactly. (*To* JEROME) Go and get dressed, darling, I'll see you later. We've got some business to settle.

JEROME *goes off into his room. The bell rings at the front door.*

VALENTINE	Oh, my God! This place is like the Gare du Nord this morning. Who can that be?

She goes to open the door and CARMAREC *bursts in.*

CARMAREC	(*Out of breath*) I ran all the way here. Can't stop. (*Seeing the two men*) Gentlemen. (*To* VALENTINE) . . . to inform you that things are hopeful. Through someone's indiscretion, I have discovered that Riccis (*Recognising the two men*) . . . ah! I see you've sorted out your problems, splendid! Yes, hm . . . well, Riccis have turned down our competitor's presentation for the perfume product. I have therefore submitted our Pefume Formula No 2, 'Love Affair'.

He is about to be when he sees JEROME.

JEROME	(*Calling out*) I say, darling, have you a hairbrush I can borrow?
VALENTINE	Yes, of course, darling, I'll be with you in a minute.
CARMAREC	Oh, God! Not another. (*To himself*) The woman's obsessed. Next time I call here I'll dress up in school uniform and try *my* luck. (CARMAREC *goes out of the flat*)
VALENTINE	Poor Carmarec. It must be all very distressing for him. (*To the two men*). I must leave you two for a moment. I've got to organise that son of mine. (VALENTINE *goes off into her room*)
GERARD	It suits me for us to be alone together for a moment.
PATRICK	Really?
GERARD	Yes, I've one or two things to ask you.
PATRICK	I swear I'll answer you truthfully.
GERARD	Right! Now, do you believe that I love Valentine?
PATRICK	Yes, I do.
GERARD	Do you believe that you love her?
PATRICK	Certainly.
GERARD	Do you believe that she believes that you love her?
PATRICK	Of course!

GERARD	And do you believe that she believes that I believe that she loves me?
PATRICK	Unquestionably.
GERARD	Good! That's got that settled, then. Now do you believe it's reasonable that Valentine loves you?
PATRICK	Reasonable? No I'm much too young for her. What can I bring into her life? My youth?
GERARD	Not for much longer.
PATRICK	Then I shall have a face lift.
GERARD	It's not funny, I have no wish to laugh.
PATRICK	There you go again, you're wrong.
GERARD	Wrong?
PATRICK	It's where you go wrong with Valentine. Lesson one. All women love to laugh, therefore you must love them with abandon, gaiety and fun.
GERARD	Not if it means prancing round on roller skates like Charlie Chaplin.
PATRICK	Then you must change your style. Gaiety, fun, adventure, that's what the ladies love. It could be a quick fling over Champagne Cocktails or eighteen months away in the Himalayas.
GERARD	Do your affairs usually last eighteen months?
PATRICK	Look Gérard. Valentine and I are enjoying a little fling, a mild flirtation. If you look up 'flirtation' in the dictionary, it says a passing fancy, like a piece of bindweed that clings to a larger, more solid love affair, like yours.
GERARD	A piece of bindweed, eh?
PATRICK	Yes, the plant, rampant but ephemeral. Here today, gone tomorrow.
GERARD	And where exactly is all this botany getting us?
PATRICK	Ah, now that's a good point. It's a question of style, Gérard. Valentine is bored with the gladioli, you must change your style. Let me look at you. A daffodil? No. A tulip? No. A pansy!

GERARD	A pansy! Now look here, young man, if you're trying to make a fool of me ...
PATRICK	Gérard, I'm trying to give you a chance. I want this to be a fair fight. Can't you understand women need an affair to be wild, insane, full of passion.
GERARD	Like a passion flower!
PATRICK	Yes, well done, you've got it! Now, show me how you would declare your love to Valentine in your new style.
GERARD	Valentine ... It's rather difficult for me in cold blood.
PATRICK	Not if you love Valentine the way she wants to be loved. Go on.
GERARD	Er, hm, Valentine, you know I'm not a man given to displays of emotion, but I'd like to say that I do appreciate you and er ...
PATRICK	That's terrible. What happened to the passion flower?
GERARD	She'll understand, I mean at our age ..
PATRICK	Stop it, it's a disaster. I'll show you. Valentine, I am wild and insane with passion for you ... Je t'adore, ma Valentine!
GERARD	That's schoolboy stuff!
PATRICK	Not if you love her, go on.
GERARD	Valentine I'm wild and insane, hm ...
PATRICK	(*Prompting him*) With passion.
GERARD	Je t'adore, ma Valentine!
PATRICK	Bravo, Gérard! Now, lesson two, you can get up off your knees if you like.
GERARD	Thank you.
PATRICK	Lesson two. All women want to be wanted.
GERARD	Yes?
PATRICK	Desired.
GERARD	Yes, yes ...

PATRICK	But never, never give them the impression of loving them.
GERARD	Never?
PATRICK	Never.
GERARD	I see, yes. Are you trying to set a trap for me?
PATRICK	Not at all Gérard. I'd be most happy to keep you on here, we seem to understand each other quite well. I'm simply giving you a fighting chance.
GERARD	All's fair in love and war, eh?
PATRICK	Absolutely.
GERARD	And what if I win and she kicks you out. What then?
PATRICK	There's a perfectly good window, I shall simply come back.
	PATRICK *leaves the flat*
VALENTINE	(*Enters followed by* JEROME) Was that Patrick just leaving?
GERARD	Yes, but don't worry he'll be back. (*To himself*) Lesson one, never give the impression of loving them. Lesson two, love them wildly, insanely, like a Passion Flower ... Oh dear.
VALENTINE	Alright then darling. You'll ask your plantation ladies to call me as soon as they get back from their little jaunt to the cemetery? I'm going to have a drink with mother Cherry Lips!
JEROME	Look here, if you're going to be insultingly rude ...
VALENTINE	As if I would. I shall wear a splendid hat covered in flowers and a dazzling smile on my face like the Duchess of York.
JEROME	Au revoir, Gérard.
GERARD	Au revoir, Jerome, and congratulations.
JEROME	Thank you. (*He goes out*)
GERARD	Now, Valentine.
VALENTINE	Now Gérard.

GERARD	Valentine, I'm not a man given to displays of emotion but I'd like to say . . .
VALENTINE	Gérard, You're not supposed to be here and as yet I have nothing to say to you.
GERARD	Well I have, Passion Flower.
VALENTINE	I beg your pardon?
GERARD	Valentine, I no longer love you.
VALENTINE	That's quite an achievement. How did you manage that?
GERARD	I've thought it out very carefully and I have to tell you that I don't love you anymore. Does that make you happy?
VALENTINE	I don't understand.
GERARD	The fact is, Valentine, that I'm a man that's not prepared to share. I'm essentially a one-woman man.
VALENTINE	You weren't in Geneva.
GERARD	That's over. In any case, I didn't *have* to tell you about that.
VALENTINE	Well, I told you about Patrick.
GERARD	Yes, and as a 'passing fancy' I might have accepted it, but it's a fancy that's not damn well passing, is it? Patrick is getting thoroughly dug in here. He's like a piece of bindweed. Well, I'm not usually shocked but . . .
VALENTINE	Yes you are and you understand nothing.
GERARD	I understand very well, that what you're after is two men in your life, at the same time.
VALENTINE	Why not? Why not three, four, five. I want to keep all the men I bump into in my life, be they colleagues, friends or lovers, it matters not. At this moment I'm experiencing the glorious feeling of being desired, if not desired, then at least loved, or maybe simply appreciated.

GÉRARD *starts to empty the cupboard of his belongings and opens his suitcase.*

GERARD   I loved you, Valentine and I appreciated you.
            Wasn't that enough?

VALENTINE   Oh, but it was, for fifteen whole years. The
            tragedy is that I only realised the day before
            yesterday that it wasn't enough any more.

GERARD   Then Patrick will have to go.

VALENTINE   No.

GERARD   Why?

VALENTINE   Because if he does, I shall suddenly grow older
            by ten years.

GERARD   That's a cruel thing to say. You and I could
            have grown old together.

VALENTINE   No thank you, not for me.

GERARD   We could have travelled, enjoyed the change of
            scene, sunshine and fresh air.

VALENTINE   I'm afraid the only air for me is the air of Paris.
            As for a change of scene, I'm quite content to
            move around this divine city, from one
            arondissement to another.

GERARD   You're ill.

VALENTINE   I was. Now, I'm convalescing and making a
            sensational recovery.

GERARD   Then you can do it on your own or with that
            damn gigolo. I don't know why I bothered to
            say that, considering I no longer love you.
            You're not the only fish in the sea. There are
            plenty of others.

VALENTINE   Oh, and are they all queuing up for you out
            there in the street?

            GÉRARD *collects his pipes, letters, books and other
            belongings and puts them into his case.*

GERARD   Besides, there's more to life than women.
            There's one's friends, one's job.

VALENTINE   And when you retire?

GERARD   There are other hobbies than women.

VALENTINE   Of course there are.

GERARD	There is love, of course.
VALENTINE	Certainly.
GERARD	Call it companionship, if you like, it's a kind of love. A man can even do without that, if he chooses to. Think of soldiers campaigning for months on end in the desert.
VALENTINE	Or fishermen on trawlers in the North Sea?
GERARD	Yes, love exists all right.
VALENTINE	Yes, it does.
GERARD	But what I have to say to you is ...
VALENTINE	What?
GERARD	Rather than lead a miserable life not finding happiness in love, it's better to give up love altogether, reject it. Get stuck into work. I'm thinking of setting up a new factory on one of those remote islands in the South Seas.
VALENTINE	What a good idea. I'm sure the natives in the South Seas are simply dying to live in ski chalets.
GERARD	I want to forget Paris altogether, and forget you. I could be happy out there on a desert island, like Robinson Crusoe.
VALENTINE	With a Girl Friday or two, no doubt.
GERARD	That's right! And a straw mattress to lie on, a sleepy lagoon under the warm sun.
VALENTINE	And any creature would be contented, dog, cat or human being, eh?
GERARD	You're making silly jokes because you don't really believe I'd ever leave you. Well, I'm sorry to disappoint you, my dear, but I shall have no difficulty whatever in doing without you. You're going to kick yourself when you see how easily I can embark on a happy life of celibacy and wipe you completely out of my thoughts, erase you totally from my memory.
VALENTINE	No need to elaborate, I've got the message.

GÉRARD *closes the suitcase he has just packed full, stuffing in a bit of shirt that got left out and is still hanging out.*

GERARD   Trouble with you women is you really believe you're indispensable. You don't think us capable of even packing a suitcase. Well, I'm going to prove to you that I can live a happy, quiet life without you. I'm laughing, ha (*He laughs falsely*) it's a big laugh. The thought of what you'll do when the day comes that you have to face up to the fact and admit that 'Gérard isn't with me any more, we're finished, washed up, he's gone'! My God, how your evenings will drag on, because you'll find that young men looking for a mother figure don't grow on trees. Once you've lost me, you'll never find another. What you'll do is to come looking for me, searching for me all over the place, 'Where is my Gérard?' But Gérard will be a long, long way across the ocean, out of the reach of scheming Parisienne career women with good noses for scent, but hearts like the hearts of artichokes. No sir! No more women for me, never again, life is too short.

VALENTINE   Life may be short, but the nights are long for a man on his own. Just think of that.

GERARD   Farewell, my dear, and the best of luck.

               GÉRARD *goes out and the door closes then it opens again, his head pops back in.*

GERARD   By the way, if you're thinking of telephoning me in Tahiti, kindly remember the time lag, I can't stand being woken up in the middle of the night!

               GÉRARD *slams out again*

VALENTINE   (*With a slight laugh to herself*) I think I know who is going to be woken up in the middle of the night. That suitcase will burst open long before he reaches the Ritz.

               PATRICK *comes in.*

PATRICK   I suspected that Gérard wanted to speak to you alone. You know me, the soul of tact. I've been

	waiting on the next floor up. (*He comes close to her*) Now its my turn ...
VALENTINE	(*Dryly*) No its not, you know.
PATRICK	What's the matter? What's happened?
VALENTINE	Nothing. Well, yes, something has. I've just had a vision in the form of a Cherry.
PATRICK	That was a symbol of good luck. A good omen for us, surely.
VALENTINE	Perhaps. All the same, Patrick dear, if you feel anything for me, any tenderness or affection whatsoever, please don't come back here for the next few days. I need to be alone for a little while. (*He tries to put his arm round her*) No, please, leave me alone, just for a time.
PATRICK	But Valentine, you can't just dismiss a man who is hopelessly knocked out by you, passionately obsessed. Don't forget that a passion like mine is like a whirlwind, it will send the branches and the leaves of the trees flying in the air, I shall be like a tornado. I shall make everything fly in the air for you. You can't send me away, you simply can't.
VALENTINE	And you have no right to use such words, my friend. 'Passionately obsessed'? Do you really know what passion is? Of course you don't. You're like a child learning to talk, using words for the first time without any idea of their meaning. Oh, my poor, poor Patrick, your passion is not even a baby's passion. (PATRICK *reacts violently*) Just be quiet for a moment and listen to me. Real passion, is like a ghastly seizure, a stoke of insanity, a terrible illness. You laugh when you should be crying, you cry when you should be laughing. You make me laugh, Patrick, but that's because you're too young to have learnt how to cry. What I call passion, is grand opera. What you're playing to me now is a pleasant and quite charming little tune on the flute. Passion is the works, it's exclusive, it devours everything. If you only

knew. You're on Gérard's side, aren't you? If
you were as passionately obsessed with me as
you say you are, you'd prove it by doing away
with Gérard, or me. Yes, that's right, you'd kill
me, because I love Gérard. That's what you
ought to do, kill me! Passionately obsessed!
Don't make me laugh! I know what passion is,
you don't.

PATRICK   You've experienced it, have you? All your life?

VALENTINE   All my life I've been waiting for a Patrick.

PATRICK   Look, if you want, I can ...

VALENTINE   No, leave me now. Do as I ask, just go, and
               leave me alone.

               PATRICK *goes out quietly.*

VALENTINE   (*To herself*) Yes, I do need to be alone. Complete
               solitude seems really rather an attractive
               prospect at the moment. At least that's what
               people say who long to be alone and never
               achieve it. It must be very pleasant to be
               entirely on one's own. Solitude, order, peace,
               silence, well, not total silence. I know myself,
               I'm dotty enough to talk to myself out loud. So
               what about reading? That's right, read a good
               book. A nice long absorbing novel, stretched out
               on the bed, and fall asleep over it. Then dream,
               what about? Then I suppose get up next
               morning, get something light for lunch ... Oh
               God, what an effort. A sandwich will do, if I'm
               alone. There won't be anyone else to think of,
               nobody to cook for, only myself. Oh God! What
               a horrible thought. Just thinking about it gives
               me the creeps. Quick, out into the street, talk to
               the first person you bump into, talk to someone,
               anyone. (VALENTINE *now mimes a conversation with
               a stranger*) Oh, excuse me, Sir, would you mind
               if I shared your table? Thank you. I see you're
               drinking beer on your own, how sad. May I join
               you. Waiter! I think I'll have a beer too. Just a
               moment, Sir, please, please, don't go, do sit
               down, I thought I might tell you (*She begins to*

cry) the story of my life it's really rather
amusing. Oh, thank you waiter, cheers. No, you
see, it's very funny, it'll make you laugh. What
happened was, that two men loved me and I
loved both of them. Oh no, don't go yet, Sir,
please stay, let me tell you my story, it's such a
fascinating, funny story ...

Slow fade-out.

Scene Two

*Lights fade up. It is a week later. 8.00 in the evening.
The table is laid elegantly with flowers and candle, as
at the beginning of the play.* VALENTINE, *in a smart
dress of lobster red silk, is putting the finishing touches
to the table. On the hatch through from the kitchen is a
superb langouste.*

VALENTINE   (*To herself*) Well, you asked for solitude, my girl,
and you've got it. (*The clock chimes*) And how!
He hasn't come, and he won't come, not any
more. (*The bell rings.* VALENTINE *smiles to herself*)
There! What am I worrying about? (VALENTINE
goes to open the door. To her surprise CARMAREC
*comes bursting in wearing pyjamas under a mackintosh.
He looks grave as he paces about the flat. Then he sits
down and puts his head in his hands. In one of his
hands he holds a telegram*). Oh my God! Carmarec,
what are you doing here? What's happened?
Have we lost the contract with Ricci?

CARMAREC   (*In a strangled voice*) On the contrary, we won it!

VALENTINE   (*Delighted*) The Love Affair project, on is it?
Then why on earth are you looking so gloomy?
You'll make a fortune out of it. What's to stop
you?

CARMAREC   My heart!

VALENTINE   Your heart? Oh, dear, I'm sorry, I didn't know.

CARMAREC   You didn't think I had a heart, did you?

VALENTINE   Of course I did. We've all got hearts. What's
the matter with yours? Have they told you?

CARMAREC	I followed your advice and told my secretary, Paulette, that I'd like to take her for a week to Mont St Michel, and do you know what she said?
VALENTINE	Didn't she fancy the place?
CARMAREC	No! I'll tell you exactly what she said. She said, 'I quite like being naughty with you at work, that's sort of like having a break for tea or a bit of time off. But to be naughty with you on a holiday, well that would spoil the holiday and make it more like being at work'.
VALENTINE	Perhaps you should go and join your wife at her ski resort in the mountains. The air would do you good.

Without a word CARMAREC *hands* VALENTINE *the telegram in his hand. She reads it out.*

VALENTINE	(*Reading*) Weather perfect. Have decided to divorce you and marry someone totally different. He's a ski instructor. Young, cheerful, strong and penniless. Hear Love Affair perfume project a success. Congratulations. You will be rich. My lawyer will contact your alimony and maintenance. Good luck! (VALENTINE *gives him back his telegram*) I take back what I said. The mountain air is not what you need at this moment. Oh, dear, poor Monsieur Carmarec. What can I do for you?
CARMAREC	You can comfort me, that's what you can do.
VALENTINE	I can't this evening. I'm expecting someone.
CARMAREC	Talking of which, how is your Romeo? Is he still in love?
VALENTINE	Yes, with Juliet's mother.
CARMAREC	I didn't have time the other day to enquire how it all went off, I mean, the meeting between your two admirers, was it alright?
VALENTINE	Thank you for your concern. Yes, it went off very well. We didn't have to call an ambulance or anything. But now you must go, Carmarec, be a dear and leave me.

CARMAREC   (*Outraged*) Valentine, how can you throw a man out into the street, who's just been betrayed by both his wife and his mistress? Have a heart. Alright, I'll admit I lied to you. The telegram came yesterday, then she came back from skiing. We had a dreadful row, and she threw me out. Oh, Valentine, let me sleep here, just for tonight.

VALENTINE   But, Carmarec ...

CARMAREC   No, please! Don't throw me out, not you too. Let me stay just for one night.

The front door bell rings.

VALENTINE   (*In a panic*) Oh, very well, you can have my son's room. Quickly, though, first door on the left. But I do not wish to see you or hear from you from now on, and you'll go tomorrow.

CARMAREC   (*About to go through to the bedroom gratefully*) Do you know what you are Valentine?

VALENTINE   (*To herself*) Yes, a soft hearted fool.

CARMAREC *disappears.* VALENTINE *puts the langouste on the table. Then a thought strikes her, as she compares it with her dress.*

VALENTINE   Snap! We're both wearing the same colour. (VALENTINE *goes to open the front door.* GÉRARD *is standing there, wearing a dinner jacket and a black tie*) What happened to your key?

GERARD   I daren't let myself in with my key. Your invitation was so formal, almost like an official summons, a Royal Command.

VALENTINE   I'd hoped you'd come, but I couldn't be certain. I thought you might be somewhere on an island in the middle of the ocean. I had to ask myself 'Does he still love me?'

GERARD   (*Helping himself to wine*) That's not your usual wine.

VALENTINE   When a woman changes, her wine changes as well.

GERARD	You may think you've changed, but, well, au fond, I suspect you're still the same person. You can't change altogether, not in a matter of days.
VALENTINE	You think? Well, you may be in for a few surprises.
GERARD	Anyway, you're in good looks this evening, my dear.
VALENTINE	That's nothing compared with the surprises I have in store for you. I've decided to have myself rolled, massaged, pummelled, stretched and slapped about like an entrecote steak, so the next time you see me I'll be a little miss in a calico dress and pigtails, and I might even have braces on my teeth.
GERARD	When I saw 'black tie' on your invitation for tonight, I thought perhaps you were giving a grand dinner party with some Government Minister coming to hang a medal on your nose for services to the perfume industry.
VALENTINE	It might well have been. We've just received a huge order for the Love Affair perfume project.
GERARD	(*Kissing her on both cheeks*) Well done! Let me honour you with two kisses. I also thought it might be your birthday and that I'd forgotten, but that's the 11th of July, isn't it?
VALENTINE	Never mind when it is, forget it. This evening we're going to celebrate our first meeting. We no longer know each other, you and I. We're strangers and I am a new Valentine you've never met before, and I would like you to do me the honour of being a brand new Gérard. You'll have to make an effort and use your imagination and your memory. You see, you've come here this evening to seduce me. We are going to play a game of rediscovery. Perhaps, it will make us feel young again, and it could be amusing. Are you on?
GERARD	(*Getting out his pipe*) Very well, Let's play your game.
	He sticks his pipe in his mouth.

VALENTINE	(*Seizing his pipe*) Ah, no! You can't just light a pipe to cover up a situation you can't deal with, pipes are forbidden. I've done with pipes. Come on, we must improvise.

GÉRARD *looks bewildered.* VALENTINE *gets out a box of cigars from a drawer and offers him one.*

VALENTINE	I've got you some Havana cigars. Here. My nose can just about stand these.
GERARD	(*Taking a cigar*) Thank you, my dear.

GÉRARD *goes over to kiss her.*

VALENTINE	No, no, no kissing that's not in the game, not yet. Its too early.

The bell rings

VALENTINE	Oh, my God, what now? (*She goes to open the door to* GHISLAINE, *who enters, weeping, and in a state of collapse*) Ghislaine, what in God's name's happened? What's the matter with you? What's the matter with this evening, it started off so well? Oh, come on, has some man made a pass at you, or what?
GHISLAINE	No such luck, would I be crying if someone made a pass at me?
VALENTINE	Well?
GHISLAINE	Its that blasted art school. Do you know what that bitch of a principal said to me? She told me I was to stop modelling for them because I had as much chance of becoming an artist as a blind orangoutang and I was wasting my time.
VALENTINE	Never mind. It's not the end of the world, go home, drink some warm milk and get yourself to bed.
GHISLAINE	Oh, please, let me stay here, it will be more cheerful for me. If I go home, all alone, I'm so afraid I'll do something silly. (*She sees* GÉRARD) Oh, good evening Monsieur Gérard. (*To* VALENTINE) Look, I'll wait at table, I'd love to. Please let me serve your dinner, it'll take my mind off things.

VALENTINE	That's very kind of you, my dear, but quite honestly we'd rather be on our own this evening.
GHISLAINE	I'll stay in the kitchen all the time, you won't see me. I'll cook your dinner and push it to you through the hatch.
VALENTINE	Our dinner is all ready, my dear, so please don't touch anything in there. Whatever you do, don't touch anything.
GHISLAINE	Well, at least let me sleep here. I'll flop down anywhere, or in here on the sofa. I'm sure Monsieur Gérard won't mind if . . .
VALENTINE	You can't flop down in here, so you'd better flop down next door.
GHISLAINE	Oh, thank you, Madame.
	GHISLAINE *rushes off.* VALENTINE *goes to the front door, flings it open and calls out into the corridor.*
VALENTINE	No more vacancies tonight, we're full. (*And she slams the door shut and turns to find* GÉRARD *sitting down to read a newspaper. She strides over and snatches the newspaper from* GÉRARD) No, Gérard. No newspapers this evening. (*She takes his hand and raises him from the chair, leading him over towards the front door*) Come on back with me, Gérard, through fifteen years of time, and try to remember the first evening we met. You came in, didn't you, to borrow an umbrella? Well, here it is Monsieur. (VALENTINE *mimes handing an umbrella to* GÉRARD) It was so kind of you to see me home, but for you I'd never would've got a taxi.
GERARD	(*Entering into the game*) My dear Madame, how exceedingly kind of you to lend me your umbrella. Are you sure you can spare it?
VALENTINE	Of course, you can bring it back some time.
	GÉRARD *turns to go, but glances as if it were out of a window.*
GERARD	That's very kind Madame, but I think the rain has stopped now.

VALENTINE	(*Taking the umbrella*) There! You never know, do you? Of course, a heavy shower can always break out when you least expect it. Very changeable, the weather, this time of year.

GÉRARD *sneezes.*

GERARD	Oh, excuse me, I think I've caught a cold.
VALENTINE	Oh dear! Shall I get a hot toddy or something? If you've got a minute.
GERARD	(*Speaking rather loud*) That's most kind of you, but don't bother about a hot toddy, a drop of cognac would do nicely.
VALENTINE	Why are you shouting?
GERARD	Because at this point, I seem to remember, you were through there in the kitchen.
VALENTINE	Yes I was, but I'm back now with a glass of brandy for you.
GERARD	What happened then, I can't remember?
VALENTINE	I stumbled on purpose, grabbed hold of you, and was careful to spill the brandy all down your shirt front. I made you take your shirt off on the pretext of drying it for you.
GERARD	Meanwhile, you unbuttoned your blouse on the pretext of not getting it wet while you washed the brandy out of my shirt. That's how I started pondering, not of what to say to you, but of what I'd like to do to you.
VALENTINE	And you did, didn't you, remember?
GERARD	I remember.

There is a long pause. Then VALENTINE *takes his hand and leads him to sit at the dinner table, and pours a glass of wine for each of them. They raise their glasses to each other, and look into each other's eyes. The door opens and* PATRICK *comes in. He walks round the table, looking at them as though they were exhibits in a wax museum.*

PATRICK	Something tells me that I've made an entrance into the wrong scene. I'm obviously not wanted

in this one. Evening dress, dinner jacket, jewellery. Where's the Champagne? Are they filming a scene for a Hollywood movie? No! It's a flashback to the 1900s. A scene from an old fashioned operetta. The last waltz, the tragic final tango. Should I creep discreetly away and leave them? No! I have a part to play in this scene. I have lines to deliver. 'Valentine, is that your lover? That rather grim-looking elderly man? But this is an outrage! I'm your lover and two lovers are one too many. So I will remove myself from the scene.' Ha. (*He laughs and stops the parody*). In point of fact I have no intention of leaving. You see, I love Valentine and I need her. You need her, too, Gérard, and she needs both of us. So what shall we do? It's not a case of squaring the circle. I know I failed in maths at school but I do know about the isosceles triangle. The base of it is Valentine, the right hand side is me, the left you, Gérard. What? You dislike being on the left? Alright I'll be on the left, you take the right. There, now everything is in order, we have a triangle. So kindly stop playing old fashioned love scenes when I'm not here. It makes me feel like a child who has not been allowed to stay up with the grown-ups.

PATRICK *pulls up a chair and sits at the table.*
VALENTINE *rises to her feet.*

GERARD   Valentine, my dear, I know you're feeling a little awkward and embarrassed but I do think that you should invite Patrick to dine with us.

VALENTINE   But ...

GERARD   But what, my dear? Surely it's what St Martin said; we must share ourselves with others. What's on the cards for two people is surely on the cards for three. Patrick, there's a glass over there. (PATRICK *goes to collect the glass, to* VALENTINE) Why are looking at me like that? Have I said something odd?

VALENTINE   (*In a strangled voice*) No.

GERARD	(*To* PATRICK) Have you dined yet, Patrick?
PATRICK	Well, no . . .
GERARD	Splendid! Neither have we. Valentine, will you rustle up a little something in the kitchen? You will, Valentine, won't you? She will.
	(VALENTINE *exists, glazed*)
GERARD	Do sit down, old chap.
PATRICK	Oh, thank you sir.
GERARD	Look, you really must stop calling me 'sir'. (*He raises his glass*) Toujours l'amour!
PATRICK	Are you trying to set a trap for me?
GERARD	Absolutely not! I'd be happy to keep you on here. This triangle thing, interesting idea.
PATRICK	Are you thinking what I think you're thinking?
GERARD	My dear chap, this is 1925. Ah, I do believe dinner is on its way.
VALENTINE	Do you both fancy some Cold Beef in Aspic?
GERARD	Madame, how I love Cold Beef in Aspic.
PATRICK	Valentine, your Cold Beef in Aspic is delicious.
VALENTINE	Good. (*She comes down stage and speaks to the audience*) This doesn't feel quite right. It should be pistols at dawn. Still, if the way to a man's heart is through his stomach, let it be Cold Beef in Aspic. But you have to admit, it's all a trifle bizarre. (VALENTINE *goes back into the kitchen*)
PATRICK	We're going skiing for Easter, you know.
GERARD	What a splendid notion! It's ages since I had on a pair of skis. I used to cut rather a dash on skis.
PATRICK	You're too late, the hotels in Zermatt are fully booked. I got the last double room, well, it's the bridal suite.
GERARD	I won't hear of it. Why waste your money on hotels when we can all stay free in one of my ski chalets. I won't take no for an answer.

PATRICK   Now look, Gérard, this was going to be just me
               and Valentine.

GERARD   But then you remembered the perfect triangle,
               eh? Besides, it's the skiing we're going for. I bet
               you roller skates are something else on the piste.

PATRICK   It's nice of you to say so. I suppose I am a bit of
               an ace on ice.

GERARD   I admit I'm a bit rusty.

PATRICK   I'll soon put you straight, sir. Here's to the
               mountain air.

GERARD   To the slippery slope.

PATRICK   To the ski.

GERARD   To the après ski.

               They pour more wine.

VALENTINE   (*Coming in again*) Well, isn't this a charming
               scene of perfect harmony. Any stranger coming
               in here would think 'what a typical middle-class
               family', mother, father and only son. I'm not
               sure about the harmony. Let me tell you,
               stranger, that Patrick here is nothing but a
               windbag, a hot-air balloon who makes me feel
               giddy; whereas Gérard, by comparison, is the
               good old Empire period armchair, a bit worn
               and worm-eaten but one which nevertheless
               should not be thrown away as junk into the
               attic. (VALENTINE *starts to go back towards the
               kitchen but stops and turns to the audience*) They're
               really rather like a music hall double-act, aren't
               they? What would that make me then, their
               agent, I suppose.

               She goes off into the kitchen.

PATRICK   Hm, hm, Gérard, I would like to propose a
               toast.

GERARD   Feel free, my dear fellow!

PATRICK   To Valentine!

GERARD   I second that, to Valentine!

PATRICK   To you, Gérard.

GERARD   Oh, too kind.

PATRICK   To Valentine and Gérard.

GERARD   No, no, to Valentine and Patrick.

PATRICK   To life!

GERARD   To love!

              Suddenly CARMAREC *appears still in his mackintosh
              and pyjamas.*

CARMAREC   To Love Affair!

              Both men spin round and look at CARMAREC.

PATRICK   Good God, what are you doing here?

GERARD   Carmarec!

CARMAREC   Where is Valentine?

GERARD   She is busy in the kitchen.

CARMAREC   Good! (*He turns as* GHISLAINE *appears beside him,
              upstage.*) Come along, Ghislaine, quickly while
              the coast's clear.

              He hurries down holding GHISLAINE's *hand. They
              cross the apartment towards the front door.*

PATRICK   Where are you two going?

CARMAREC   (*Pausing at the front door*) To buy a pair of greasy
              dungarees. Then we're off to spend a naughty
              weekend together at Mont St Michel. That's
              right, isn't it, Ghislaine?

GHISLAINE   That's right. And you can tell Madame
              Matignon I won't be here next Thursday or
              Saturday or Tuesday or Friday.

CARMAREC   Come, my love!

              CARMAREC *and* GHISLAINE *go off.*

GERARD   (*Slowly*) Tuesday, Thursday, Saturday.

PATRICK   Monday, Wednesday, Friday.

GERARD   Old St Martin.

PATRICK   That's right. Share and share alike.

GERARD   Suits me.

PATRICK	Suits me.
GERARD	And on the seventh day God rested.
PATRICK	I always play golf on Sundays.
GERARD	Really? Quite extraordinary, so do I.
PATRICK	I'd be delighted to give you a game, any Sunday.
GERARD	Every Sunday. (*They raise their glasses and drink to this*).
PATRICK	Every Sunday.
GERARD	It's all settled, then.
PATRICK	That's right. Monday, Wednesday, Friday — me.
GERARD	Tuesday, Thursday, Saturday — me.
PATRICK	And Sunday, golf.
GERARD	My putting's pretty good, but I need to work on my drive.
PATRICK	Don't worry, I can always give you a few strokes.

At this point, VALENTINE *comes in from the kitchen with a dish which she sets down before them. They both start to eat.*

VALENTINE	Here you are, dinner is served. You're a couple of big spoilt babies, both of you! (*To herself*) Both of them, keep them both. All the time unless ... unless ...
PATRICK	(*Softly*) Monday, Patrick.
GERARD	(*Softly*) Tuesday, Gérard.
PATRICK	(*Softly*) Wednesday, Patrick.
GERARD	(*Softly*) Thursday, Gérard.
VALENTINE	Friday, Patrick, Saturday, Gérard and Sunday?

At this moment, there is a ring on the bell. VALENTINE *goes over to open the front door. Standing there is a young man holding a bouquet of flowers.*

YOUNG MAN	Madame Matignon?
VALENTINE	Yes?

YOUNG MAN   (*Handing the bouquet*) For you, special delivery.

VALENTINE   Oh, thank you, how sweet of you.

YOUNG MAN   My pleasure, Madame.

The young man turns to go. VALENTINE watches him with the slightest look of regret. Then she slaps her own wrist in self rebuke and turns backs into the apartment. She crosses over past the two men, looking at the bouquet and looking at them each in turn. As she looks at them, they both shake their heads to deny having ordered the flowers. She comes down stage, looks and finds a card in the bouquet, then she looks out front at the audience. She seems to spot a face in the stalls and fixes her eyes on it.

VALENTINE   Thank you very much indeed, sir, how charming of you. I'd love to. May I suggest next Sunday?

The two men on the stage react with horror. Blackout.

THE CURTAIN FALLS

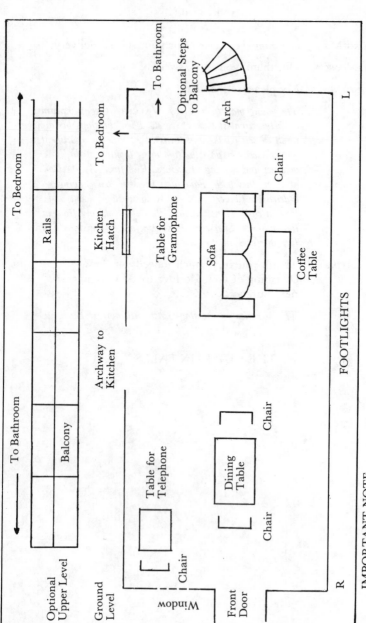

Optional Upper Level

Ground Level

To Bathroom

Balcony

To Bedroom

Rails

Table for Telephone

Window

Chair

Archway to Kitchen

Dining Table

Chair

Chair

Front Door

Kitchen Hatch

To Bedroom

Table for Gramophone

Optional Steps to Balcony

To Bathroom

Arch

Sofa

Coffee Table

Chair

FOOTLIGHTS

R

L

IMPORTANT NOTE

The use of an upper level, as in the original production at the Theatre Royal, Brighton, is optional. The play can be performed on one level, with the bedroom and bathroom exits upstage left, as indicated.

from the original Thorndike Theatre Production

ENGLISH THEATRE GUILD LTD.
PLAY AGENTS AND PUBLISHERS

Also available from ETG, Alfred Shaughnessy's latest thriller, DOUBLE CUT, adapted from the film CHASE A CROOKED SHADOW.

An ingenious new thriller set in a luxury villa on the Costa del Sol. The plot revolves around diamond heiress Olivia Prescott whose villa is disturbed by an enigmatic stranger claiming to be her supposedly dead brother. He seems to know every trivial detail of their past family life, his papers verify his identity, but Olivia insists with mounting hysteria that he is an imposter. He manages to convince all around him with the exception of Olivia and we begin to question whether Olivia herself is not concealing something. The plot thickens when we learn that £10 million worth of diamonds are missing. It this what the stranger is after? The complications are finally unravelled in a revealing denouement to a taut and well-written thriller.

For further information, contact,

ETG,
English Theatre Guild Ltd,
129 Park Street,
London W1Y 3FA